OF PEATS AND PUTTS

A WHISKY AND GOLF TOUR OF SCOTLAND

ANDREW BROWN

YOUCAXTON PUBLICATIONS

OXFORD & SHREWSBURY

ISBN 978-1-912419-16-6
Printed and bound in Great Britain.
Published by YouCaxton Publications 2018
YCBN 002.1

YouCaxton Publications
enquiries@youcaxton.co.uk

For my fellow members of

The Longshanks Golfing Society

Acknowledgements

I AM INDEBTED to many friends, colleagues, golfing and whisky-drinking companions who have encouraged me in my venture into book writing. However, there are two people without whom this book would not have succeeded: Alice Young, my niece, who edited my manuscript and provided invaluable advice on content and structure, and Christine Laffan, whose wonderful illustrations have helped bring alive the many beautiful places which I visited.

About the Author

Andrew Brown was born in Edinburgh, brought up in the Borders and educated at Loretto School in Musselburgh. After reading history at Cambridge University, specialising in British political and social history of the seventeenth and eighteenth centuries, he pursued a career in the food industry and was involved in the marketing of many household names such as Bisto, Hovis and Mr Kipling. His interest in both golf and whisky has evolved over the years. He is now retired with three grown-up children, and pays regular visits to Scotland to indulge his passion. He lives in the Chilterns and, apart from golf, he is an enthusiastic dog walker, a very average tennis player and a novice gardener.

Contents

Acknowledgements   vi

Preface   ix

Chapter 1:   Sutherland   1

Chapter 2:   Cromarty   17

Chapter 3:   Moray   33

Chapter 4:   Speyside   47

Chapter 5:   Perthshire   61

Chapter 6:   The Kingdom Of Fife   75

Chapter 7:   East Lothian   91

Chapter 8:   Kintyre   107

Chapter 9:   Islay   123

Afterword   137

Foretaste   145

Preface

WHY 'WHISKY AND golf'? (It could as easily have been 'golf and whisky' but somehow the former scans better). Well, they are Scotland's two gifts to the world. It is not as if they are inextricably linked but they do have a lot in common. They were both invented in Scotland, are strongly associated around the world with Scotland, and are playing an increasingly important part in Scotland's economy. In many other ways, however, they are quite distinct; for example, within Scotland they do not really share the same geography. Speyside is often regarded as the heart of the Scottish whisky industry but here great golf courses are a little sparse. Equally, Fife is probably the richest area for golf in Scotland, having nearly 50 courses, but until recently there were no malt whisky distilleries within 'the kingdom'.

I should start by managing expectations. If you are looking for either a definitive history of the Scottish whisky industry or a new guide to the best golf courses in Scotland, you will be disappointed. My qualifications are not up to either task and others have already done both very successfully. I am a proud Scot, though one who has spent the last 35 years south of the border. I am a keen but average golfer and an occasional whisky drinker. I do not profess to be an expert on either subject. My interest in both is that of the enthusiastic amateur with a pride that Scotland has offered the world these two great leisure pursuits; whisky drinking and golfing.

This tour of Scotland encompasses visits to nine distilleries and nine golf courses. I chose nine as it is a peculiarly golfing number. I have tried for a geographical spread across Scotland and managed to include all the most important whisky and golfing areas, though perhaps the Ayrshire coast is a gap in terms of great golfing destinations. My purpose has been to discover more about the country of my birth and my childhood, but also learn more about how whisky and golf developed in Scotland before they both became popular worldwide.

I wanted to discover what connects these iconic Scottish industries and pastimes. I can see similarities, perhaps accidental or contrived, but is there some innate, distinctive 'Scottishness' that has made them? Is it a coincidence that both developed strongly in the late 19th century? I am curious to learn how they have evolved, how they became popular throughout the world, and how, in future, they can perhaps learn from each other. I felt that only by visiting a wide selection of golf clubs and distilleries in different areas of Scotland with these questions in mind, could I begin to find some answers.

Scotland has been an inspiration for both golf and whisky around the world. Golf started in Scotland and when interest took off in the United States it was often Scottish course architects who designed the early layouts. It is impossible to underestimate the influence of Scottish designers on the major American courses, many of which are used for the US Open today. Indeed a history of golf course architecture starts in Scotland with many of the modern designers all around the world now returning to the original principles established by the likes of Old Tom Morris and James Braid, whose courses provide six of the nine I have chosen. So too in whisky, though here it was visitors taking back their experience to their own countries. The person most often associated with the founding of the now renowned Japanese whisky industry, Masataka Taketsuru, learned his trade in Scotland, attending Glasgow University and even marrying a Scot. There is less evidence of the influence of Scots on the American whiskey (yes, in America, as in Ireland, it is whiskey and not whisky) and Bourbon industries; indeed many Scots would not want these drinks closely compared!

What interests me about whisky and golf? I think three things in particular are important; location, history and 'architecture'. These three factors are also inter-connected. The nine golf courses which I cover are by no means the best or most famous nine in Scotland. Some are famous, others not. The same is true of the distilleries; some make internationally renowned brands, others are less well known. The choices are personal and in the course of my research I have changed my mind several times. But all the courses are ones that can be played for a reasonable Green Fee and enjoyed by mid and high handicap golfers alike, while all the distilleries welcome visitors. I have looked for courses and distilleries which are geographically proximate (as I mentioned above this was not always easy) and, while seldom is there any direct link between the two, I wanted to discover whether particular locations or landscapes have had similar influences. The selection offers a broad cross section of what Scotland can offer in whisky drinking and golfing enjoyment. I have started in the north, in Sutherland, and the course of the book takes the form of a tour southwards ending on the lovely island of Islay in the southern Hebrides. As well as each of the regions having particular characteristics, each individual distillery will have its own distinctive features, often a consequence of either its location or history. Admittedly seven of the nine courses are 'links', but I think that is a fair representation of what Scotland provides in golfing excellence and this does not make them all the same. I have deliberately excluded the famous courses on The Open rota as these need considerable notice to book and have become very expensive.

History is also important to me. Just as when I visit a new country or city I want to know more about its history and how it has developed over the years, so too when visiting a golf course I want to know when, and by whom, it was built and designed and how the club started. With whisky, there is not only the history of when each distillery was set up and any changes in ownership, but the changing nature of the market it serves; the huge growth in the industry in recent years has in many ways been driven by demand from newly affluent Asian consumers. This has had, and will continue to have, major impacts on the distilleries. Already they recognise the need to design and offer a wide array of product varieties to satisfy this new and lucrative market.

This brings me to architecture; the design of the product and the courses. This is a subject that fascinates me. As in all things, there are clearly design trends in golf courses which can make one course very different from another. One of the joys of golf is that every course is different. A tennis court or a football pitch, whether it is in Scotland, England, Europe, America or Asia, is essentially the same. The surface and weather conditions may vary but otherwise that is it. Every golf course, however, is unique and design is a major factor in any course. The design will be strongly influenced by both the location and the history, i.e. where it is and when it was built. I have a strong preference for the natural over the contrived and this has heavily influenced my choices. I am a particular fan of courses in beautiful locations, where the course is an intrinsic part of that location so that the golfing experience is about more than the course itself. Good designs recognise this. I have managed also to feature a cross section of the great course designers here, from Old Tom Morris and Willie Park Junior to James Braid, Alister Mackenzie and Harry Colt.

Just as with golf courses, every whisky is different. The Islay malts are very different from the Highland ones and these characteristics are generally a combination of local conditions and product design. Just as the landscape of the locality is a major factor in the style of golf course design, so too is it a heavy influence on the type of whisky produced. The water used, and the soil itself, can have an impact on the taste of the whisky. Some whiskies will use local peat to impart flavour; peat is more associated with the wetter weather conditions in the west rather than the dryer, colder east. The soil is an enormous factor in any golf course, whether links, heathland or parkland. So too with the weather; as we will see, on links courses, the wind is very much a part of the course's defence and its location, be it on the east coast or west coast, with their differing prevailing winds, has a major impact on the course and its design. A well-designed links course will generally try to have a range of holes facing different directions so that the player has to play shots with the wind behind, into the wind, as well as coping with a left to right and a right to left wind. An inland course is more likely to have trees, which often become an integral part of course designs and also play a role in funnelling wind.

I can think of other similarities between whisky and golf. Both offer more in their enjoyment than might be supposed of a simple walk and a drink. There is a philosophy to both, a ceremony, a communion. I acknowledge that being an advocate of golf as a noble pastime is hardly novel. I understand the 'good walk spoiled' notion but here I will put up a strong defence. It is in my mind a great sport which enables good exercise for all ages and can genuinely be enjoyed from 8 to 80. There is much of life in golf. There are rules (some of which are certainly somewhat crass) and there is an understanding that you play by these rules, even if at times they seem unfair. There is also that thing called etiquette. Good manners and courtesy, things which I think society today could certainly benefit from more of. Good golfing etiquette is not only good manners but also common sense, and contributes to everyone being better off. It is about respect and a sense of community. Golfing etiquette is focused on each individual being aware of others; not walking across the line of their putt, playing in turn, leaving your bag next to the green in the direction of the next hole so that you don't hold up others behind. It is all simple, common sense; little things which can make a big difference.

I believe that there is also a calmness and courtesy about malt whisky drinking. This is a drink that should not be drunk in a hurry. It is certainly a product that is not made in a hurry. Like golf, Scotch whisky has strict rules; only three ingredients are permitted and there are regulations as to how, and how long, it must be matured to be called Scotch whisky. The premium malts often have a maturation of at least 10 years; malt whisky has to respect traditions and aim to be timeless. It therefore attracts a particular audience and here the overlap with a discerning golf enthusiast who respects the traditions of the game is clear. This is reflected in the marketing of the product – whisky advertisements are never brash or controversial but generally calm and restrained in tone in contrast to, say, lager or vodka.

Somehow whisky has become more than just another drink. Not only are there a remarkable number of books published on whisky but it has attracted much debate, discussion, writing and poetry over the years, a sense that it is more than merely that combination of three ingredients and time, just as golf is more than just getting the ball into the hole. There is that other element, that inexplicable something that makes the sum of its parts and the weight of tradition into so much more than a drink. When you drink a whisky you are part of something. That weight of history and tradition behind you, allows you to be uniquely and paradoxically alone while part of an inherent community, one that is infused into the very liquid itself. You are partaking in something more than a drink and you are in company with generations of makers and drinkers, with those that have used the land, with those who have passed through it.

Golf is also special in that a professional can have a proper game with an amateur. I could not play Roger Federer at tennis or face Andrew Flintoff's bowling at cricket. To play with me they would not be able to play their normal game. The elite play a different game. In golf, however, the handicap system enables everyone to have a real contest. And, even more special, if Rory McIlroy and I had the same shot from, say, 120 yards to a green, occasionally I will play the better shot. The difference between Rory McIlroy and me is that 9 times out of 10 (OK, maybe 99 times out of a 100!) he will play the better shot. But, delightfully, perhaps one time out of ten, I might. How special would that feel? Yes, occasionally as an amateur you will play the perfect shot, a shot which would beat a professional. I don't think this is true in many sports.

This democracy is also present in whisky. From its origins as an illicit distilled product in traditional highland farming communities, to the broad appeal it has today, whisky has never been just an 'elite' product. There has also always been a wide range of distilleries with different ownerships and while, like any industry, there has been consolidation, it is good still to see many long-established private family businesses and an increasing number of smaller 'micro-distilleries'. So the industry is quite diverse and not dominated by big brands managed by rich multi-national companies. Just as in golf the amateur can compete alongside the professional, smaller operations can compete with the big brands. The success of a whisky is not generally about 'low cost production' and I have included a wide range of distillery types to reflect this.

Finally I believe there is also a spiritual side to both golf and whisky. It seems to me that both allow us space in our lives to pause, to reflect. Both encourage thought, concentration, and calmness. It is that which makes me wonder, of what are these moments made? What mysterious element is added to both that gives each its unique place? Perhaps I am biased, perhaps returning home always has that feeling for me, but I can't help but feel it might be Scotland herself. This is not to say you can't enjoy golf anywhere else, or extol the virtues of a Japanese malt, but these two great things reflect the Scotland I know, its respect for landscape, for history and tradition.

We are all searching for spiritual well-being and for me probably I am happiest when;

- It is perhaps 6.30pm on a May evening in Scotland.
- I am playing a links course.
- The light is sharp, yet with a slight twinkle – only those who have experienced the particular evening light you get on links courses will fully understand what I mean.
- I am walking up a fairway amidst some dunes alongside the sea and you can see the beach and coastline.
- It is sunny and pleasantly warm (but not hot).
- The skylarks are in full song.

There is a breeze – probably a one club breeze (for non-golfers this means you have to use a club one lower [bigger, yes, I know it is confusing] than you would otherwise have done if there had been no wind).

I am playing well! Yes, this makes a difference, although it is probably the least important factor on my list. I would want to be playing well and I would want also to be playing well against a friend in a match which is competitive – golf is enjoyed much better if it is played in a spirit of strong but friendly competition.

It is in these moments I have found real happiness and life satisfaction. Golf, like life, can also be infuriating and frustrating. You can play well one day and not the next. It can also be unfair. You can be unlucky. Dealing with these ups and downs is a mental challenge and how successfully you meet this challenge will determine how good you become. This is also a lesson in life, as the manner in which you deal with the inevitable highs and lows will determine how you lead your life.

A late night drink of malt whisky too is a time for contemplation and therefore best consumed after an enjoyable day, perhaps one where I have experienced a delightful round of links golf as described above. But it can also be a time for more melancholic contemplation, perhaps again at life's ups and downs, and a glass of whisky can help put matters into perspective.

Let us leave the philosophy and start the tour.

Clynelish
Brora
Dunrobin Castle
Glenmorangie
Tain
Benromach
Moray
Glenlivet
Carrbridge
Inverness
Boat of Garten
Aberdeen
Edradour
Blairgowrie
Dundee
Eden
Daftmill
Anstruther
Bass Rock
Bunnahabhain
Edinburgh
Kilspindie
Machrie
Glasgow
Glenkinchie
Machrihanish
Springbank
Dunaverty

Brora Golf Club

This magnificent view from the clubhouse changes dramatically with the seasons: in May the hills will be almost dazzlingly yellow with the gorse; in autumn they will be vibrantly purple with heather. The sea will also change colour from the brightest blue to the deepest grey.

Clynelish; the Old Distillery

Old Clynelish is an archetypal old Scottish distillery with its stone walls and slate roof with a pagoda-style top to the old malting kilns. The brick chimney shows that this is an industrial scene though the setting is rural as distilleries would always be situated near to a natural water source.

CHAPTER ONE

Sutherland

'We borrowed golf from Scotland as we borrowed whisky.
Not because it is Scottish but because it is good'

Horace Hutchison (1859-1932)

English Amateur golfer and first English Captain of
the Royal and Ancient Golf Club

WE WILL VISIT many beautiful places in this book (as I said in the preface, I like golf to be played in beautiful surroundings) but Brora is a candidate for the most majestic.

About halfway from Inverness to John O'Groats, it is a fitting place to start a tour of Scotland as it offers so much of what Scotland has; a proud history, spectacular scenery and great whisky and golf. The whisky comes from the town's Clynelish distillery and the golf from the Brora Golf Club, one of James Braid's (we will come across him a lot!) famous creations and indeed the headquarters of the James Braid Golfing Society. The history is provided by the Sutherland family; the imposing statute of the 1st Duke of Sutherland on the top of Ben Bhraggie can be viewed from the Brora course while the clan's ancestral home, Dunrobin Castle, is the other main local visitor attraction just down the road in Golspie.

There are golf courses and indeed distilleries further north both in Orkney (the famous Highland Park) and on the mainland (Old Pulteney is in Wick) but I think Brora is the first place where two significant ones combine. As Clynelish is, at the moment (see below), the only distillery in Sutherland it is a natural choice. For golf, Golspie could make a claim; it is an enjoyable course but not as 'classic' -I will explain what I mean by that in due course- as Brora. As well as some fine links holes along the sea, it has three holes around the turn which move into pine forests and are very 'heathland' in feel, while some of the later holes have a 'parkland' appearance. It is a good course but without the distinctiveness of Brora. The clubhouse (an important part of the golfing experience) is functional but no more than that. The town of Golspie, however, is actually rather prettier than Brora which, apart from the area around the golf course, rather disappoints.

Brora is a town with an industrial past with, as well as whisky distilling, coal mining, salt panning, tweed production and electricity generation all previously being thriving activities. The existence of these industries is inextricably linked with the Sutherland family, which dominated the history of the area. The Earldom of Sutherland was created in 1235 and is one of the seven ancient earldoms of Scotland and the site of the ancestral home, Dunrobin Castle, dates from this time. The Sutherland family throughout its history was always very influential politically, generally from the Protestant tradition and supporting the British government in standing up against the Jacobite risings. In the early 19th century, the earldom was held by the Countess of Sutherland who married George Leveson-Gower, the Marquis of Stafford, who just six months before his death was given a peerage and created the 1ˢᵗ Duke of Sutherland. The Countess was closely associated with the controversial 'highland clearances' involving the forced eviction of small tenant farmers to make way for more profitable sheep farming. The Sutherlands' plan was to resettle the population in coastal towns and it was this which prompted the new industries of coal mining, distilling and salt panning. It was, allegedly, a form of benevolent social engineering but took little notice of the wishes of those affected while some of the eviction methods were quite brutal. Thus the episode, even today, leaves an uncomfortable legacy.

Dunrobin Castle

Dunrobin Castle lies just north of Golspie and is definitely worth a visit; the Sutherland family history explains much about the area and the castle and its grounds are magnificent. While the site has been the home to the Sutherlands since the 13ᵗʰ century, the look of the castle today dates from about 1845, when

Sir Charles Barry, who had designed the Houses of Parliament, was commissioned to turn it into a baronial home. Subsequently, after a serious fire in 1915, the famous Scottish architect, Robert Lorimer, made changes to some of the exterior and completely refurbished the interiors. The castle, with its towers, has a French feel to it while the gardens, which Barry also designed, were inspired by those at Versailles. Today visitors are also treated to an impressive falconry display while plans have been submitted for a distillery to be built in a former powerhouse in the castle grounds so Clynelish will have a local competitor.

The Clynelish distillery is situated about a mile north of the town of Brora and is nestled at the bottom of a valley about a mile from the main road. We will visit many different distilleries in this trip; some large, some small, some old and some new, some owned by big multi-national businesses and others which remain small local enterprises. Clynelish is owned by Diageo which operates nearly 30 distilleries and has a market share of Scotch whisky in excess of 30 per cent. We will come across them again in Chapter 7 at Glenkinchie. Diageo is today's manifestation of one of the most famous companies in the history of Scotch whisky, dating back to the formation of The Distillers Company in 1877 which combined six whisky companies. The Distillers Company gradually acquired other distilleries through its history until it was bought in 1986 by Guinness in one of the most controversial takeovers in UK corporate history, with four businessmen subsequently found guilty of artificially inflating the Guinness share price to see off an alternative bidder. The business was combined with another distiller, Arthur Bell and Sons, to become United Distillers, before Diageo was formed some ten years later creating a multinational drinks business.

Diageo may be a big multinational company but, with its history in whisky, it understands that the future for malt whisky lies in its differences rather than in its uniformity. It has deliberately bought distilleries in different areas producing very distinctive products and has indeed made a marketing initiative of a 'malt whisky flavour map' of its range of brands in each of the whisky regions to help inform its customers of their specific characteristics. It markets its brands together under the umbrella of 'the Classic Malts Collection'. As in this book we will explore different geographies of Scotland, we will naturally therefore come across contrasting product types from the 'peaty' malts of Islay to the much more mild Lowland malts.

The history of whisky making at Clynelish is long and complicated. There are actually two distilleries here. The original distillery was founded in 1819 by, inevitably, the Sutherlands as part of the plan to create new employment for resettled crofters. It had various owners throughout the 19th century before being acquired by Distillers in 1912. The distillery was mothballed in 1931 as the industry suffered from the effects of prohibition before production re-started in 1939. In 1967 a new distillery was built next door and the old one was again mothballed the following year. Then, just a year later, the old distillery was re-opened and named the Brora Distillery, producing a distinctive, peaty single malt. The distillery was then again closed in 1983. Diageo still own a small amount of stocks of Brora whisky which are released and sold to collectors; a 40 year old was released in 2014 at a retail price of £7,000 a bottle.

Clynelish is a major producer of whisky for the Johnny Walker brand and as such is an important site in the Diageo portfolio. Indeed Diageo has announced that significant investment will take place at the site in order to double its capacity from its current level of about 5 million litres a year. This is perhaps surprising as such a remote distillery must incur increased transport costs but Diageo believes that the product produced at Clynelish is distinctive (the word 'waxy' is used by experts) so are not prepared to risk attempting to replicate producing the same product elsewhere.

The single malt is produced under the Clynelish brand with a 14-year -old as the main line. The distillery has a modest visitor centre and tours are available around what is quite a simple site. The new distillery building is unremarkable but the old buildings of the Brora distillery next door are attractive. However, within the new distillery they have recognised its delightful location and created a large window in the main still room from where you get a magnificent view across to the coast. The tour is very informal yet informative and ends with a tasting. Do I detect the 'waxiness' that they claim as distinctive? It is smooth; it is pleasant. I can taste the difference between the three drams offered but I am still struggling to articulate what those differences are. I clearly need more practice.

It is a good place to start a tour of distilleries and pose the questions which I will explore; what makes one whisky different from another and how is it that a product with just three permitted ingredients (malted barley, water and yeast) can have so many different manifestations? A bit like golf, the essential elements of whisky making are all the same and indeed regulated, yet the end results can be a world apart.

Here is a very quick guide to malt whisky making. The dried and milled, malted barley is put into a 'mash tun' (a large vessel) with water added at different temperatures. Each distillery has very strong and precise views as to what these temperatures should be. The 'mashing' allows the starches to break down into sugars and form a liquid called 'wort'. This is transferred to a 'wash back' (another large vessel!) where yeast is added and fermentation takes place over an extended period of days to produce a beer-like liquid called 'pot ale' which is then ready for distilling.

There are then two types of still. The initial 'pot still' is where the pot ale is distilled and then passed through a condenser to produce 'low wines' increasing the alcoholic content from the 7-9 per cent of the pot ale to over 20 per cent. These 'low wines' are then distilled again in the 'spirit still' to produce the end spirit which is generally between 60 and 70 per cent proof. It is this which is then put into barrels for maturation. By law this has to be for at least three years, though for most classic malts it will be from 10 to 12 years.

That is very much a potted summary of the whisky distilling process. What is interesting is how each distillery will point to slight differences in its process which lead to specific characteristics in the whisky; the water, the temperature of the water, the malting of the barley, the use or not of peat in the kiln, the type of yeast, the time left in the 'wash back', the size and shape of the stills etc. etc. There is considerable mystique attached to all these elements though most will acknowledge that the single biggest factor is the nature of the maturation; in what type of barrels and for how long the whisky is matured. We will discuss this further as the tour progresses.

Brora Golf Club is only about two miles away occupying the land by the coast to the north of the town. As you progress with this book you will notice my preference for links golf (seven out of the nine courses) and the natural experience which links courses offer. The definition of a proper 'links' is not just that it is on the coast, but that the land has been reclaimed from the sea. It is this which produces the distinctive turf which is such an essential part of links golf. Most coastal courses are not actually true 'links'; for example clifftop courses are, by definition, not links though often they have similar characteristics. Brora delivers a classic example of a true links course, designed and laid out on a piece of pure 'linksland' and uses that land to best effect. It also uses the other elements; the coastline and, of course, the weather, as this stretch of coast is never short of a breath of wind. That too is the beauty of a links course; you can play it in the morning and then find by the afternoon that it is completely different if the wind direction, or indeed the weather conditions generally, have changed.

I will start with a few words about James Braid whose design this is and who will feature again later at both Boat of Garten and Blairgowrie. He was one of the foremost designers of the early part of the century and designed courses all over the UK. Born in Fife in 1870, he turned professional in 1894, going on to win The Open Championship five times. He was one of what became known as 'The Great Triumvirate' (Braid, Harry Vardon and J H Taylor) who between them won The Open Championship sixteen times in the twenty years before the start of the Great War in 1914. He retired in 1908 to become Secretary of Walton Heath in Surrey and became a course designer. Over two hundred UK courses bear his mark either in terms of the original design or a substantial redesign.

The original course opened in 1891 and was a 9 hole layout built by locals. The Secretary of nearby Dornoch, John

Sutherland, (I think the name is not a coincidence) then designed a second 9 holes and some alterations were the made after a visit by J H Taylor. But it was a redesign by James Braid in 1921 which is the course we play today.

The setting is beautiful; from the clubhouse, which occupies a lofty position, you can see almost the whole course which sweeps northwards up the coastline. It is a totally natural piece of links that barely looks like a golf course. In few places are nature and golf so in harmony; so much so that to this day cattle graze on the course, with the greens being protected by low level wire fences. This may seem odd and inappropriate to the average golfer (American visitors find it incomprehensible) but at Brora it seems quite natural and in no way reduces the enjoyment of the course. Golf is a game governed by many rules, some of which are quite esoteric. The Rules of Golf are determined by The Royal and Ancient Club at St Andrews and also allow for local rules to deal with local conditions. Within the normal rules of golf if there is a puddle on the course caused by rain, this is called 'casual water' and you are allowed to move your ball with no penalty. At Brora there is a local rule entitled 'Animal Droppings' which 'may be treated as casual water'.

Livestock of some sort on golf courses is not unique to Brora; Westward Ho! in Devon, one of the oldest courses in England, still has sheep grazing and I remember when I was playing at my home course in Melrose in the Borders of Scotland in the 1970s, there were also regularly sheep on the course. More recently I have come across other examples. At Lahinch, on the west coast of Ireland, there are the famous two white goats which have now become the club emblem. The original goats belonged to a caddie around the turn of the 20th century but there remain two handsome ones which roam the course today. Apparently they also serve a useful function in terms of predicting the weather; if they are found sheltering in the dunes near the clubhouse the prospects are poor whereas if they are seen heading out towards the coast, players can be reassured that the weather is on an improving trend. I have also experienced more exotic animals; at Barnbougle Dunes, a wonderful new links course on the North East coast of Tasmania, you are accompanied on the front nine in particular by numerous wallabies. They are reserved but friendly, either sitting in the long rough or occasionally gathering around the greens where they observe the play. Nothing, however, compares with the experience at Minchinhampton in Gloucestershire. Golf has been played here on the common for over 125 years making it one of England's older courses. The main club has now moved a few miles away where two impressive new courses have been built. The Old Course, however, set on the beautiful high common with wonderful views in almost every direction, is a unique experience. There are no bunkers but it is the site of many Neolithic and Bronze Age burial mounds, so the landscape has plenty of character. In terms of livestock it is not a case of the odd roaming beast; there are veritable herds of cattle, comfortably outnumbering golfers, exercising ancient grazing rights at particular times of year on land now managed by the National Trust. At times it is like playing in front of galleries of spectators. They generally keep to the rough (though here the distinction between rough and fairway is, it has to be said, a little blurred) and their etiquette is generally good; their expressions usually passive and unimpressed. Many are big beasts and they are remarkably placid, though at times some of the young calves can get a little frisky and run across the fairway. A local rule again provides for (how shall I put this delicately?) you getting a 'sticky' lie, and rubber gloves are strongly recommended as an additional accessory in your golf bag. It all adds to the occasion; golf being played in the context of its surroundings rather than golf for its own sake. To me that is how it should be.

Returning to Brora, the course is a Par 70 with four Par 3s and just two par 5s, but to the amateur golfer the number of effective Par 5s will depend on how much wind there is. There are five Par 4s of over 400 yards, which if they are into the prevailing wind, are effective 'three – shotters' (i.e. the number of shots it takes to reach the green from the tee) for the average golfer. And wind there usually is! Weather is usually a crucial factor at Brora and there is generally a lot of it, with the high mountains falling steeply to the coast. It is very possible to start the round in gentle sunny weather with a light breeze and find that by the 9th hole the wind is gusting above 25mph with ominous clouds looming – that was exactly what happened when I last played it. We set off at lunchtime in benign conditions – the impression was of a gentle test of golf to follow. After a couple of holes the wind gradually started to strengthen and by the time we were heading back on the second nine it was a full-blown gale and the course was anything but gentle. Such is links golf.

The design is a classic 'out and back' links with the first nine holes heading out along the coast and the back nine heading back alongside on the inland side of the links. With the coastline facing south-east, generally the prevailing wind is from the west so the course requires handling a left to right wind on the way out and a right to left on the way in. Adjusting halfway is one of the challenges of playing links golf. Somehow at Brora the wind never quite seems to be directly behind and helping, except perhaps at the very short Par 3, 13th where you don't want it! There is really only one hole on each nine which faces across the links, these being the Par 3s, 6 and 13. The terrain is very natural, undulating linksland. The turf is very good and greens are high quality, with traditional deep pothole bunkers. There are two burns (Scottish for stream) and one is in play at four holes adding extra interest. All the Par 3s are memorable; the 6th is a 200 yard shot facing directly inland to a well-protected, elevated green; the 9th is a gentle downhill shot at the far end of the course to a green sitting just above the beach; the 13th is a very short hole played across the burn requiring good judgement of distance and, unusually, the final Par 3 is the last hole, a tough uphill 200 yard shot towards the clubhouse and usually into the prevailing wind. My favourite hole? At Brora there isn't one which stands out – the Par 3 6th is a good looking hole as is the short 9th; perhaps the 17th with the elevated tee looking back towards the clubhouse? There is certainly not an uninteresting hole at Brora.

There are many other features on the course apart from the constant, stunning views. The club logo is an arctic tern and there is a protected colony which nests on the beach alongside the course. For those who know their birds there are, in addition to the ever present skylarks, ringed plovers, oystercatchers, sand martins and even fulmars. Out at sea it is not unusual to see harbour porpoises, bottlenose dolphins and otters. Truly golf and nature combine very naturally at Brora.

The clubhouse has been renovated somewhat in recent years and, with the club celebrating its 125th anniversary in 2016, it has a new club logo and a well-equipped shop. The food in the clubhouse is honest golfing fare and the welcome is friendly. One potentially disappointing factor is the proposal to build a windfarm on a hill above the coastline to the north of the club which will spoil what is a magnificently natural view.

Brora delivers everything a good golf course should; a tough but enjoyable test for all levels of players, in delightful surroundings with a welcoming clubhouse. These will be my criteria for choosing the subsequent courses.

Tain Golf Club; 11th green

This view of 11th green from the 12th tee encapsulates everything about
Tain in one scene. In fact very little of the course borders the sea but
here you can see the Dornoch Firth as well as the thick wooded area
which is an unusual feature on a links course but a feature of Tain.

Old Tom Morris

This extraordinary wooden statue was carved out of the trunk of an old tree which overlooked the first tee by a local craftsman. Old Tom's somewhat dour expression greets visitors as they drive into the car park.

CHAPTER TWO

Cromarty

*'Whisky, no doubt, is a devil; but why has
this devil so many worshippers?'*

Lord Henry Cockburn (1779-1854)

Solicitor General for Scotland

THE JOURNEY TO our next location is probably
the shortest within this book. The Royal Burgh of
Tain is less than an hour south of Brora just after
you have crossed the Dornoch Firth. However, I
strongly recommend a detour off the A9 from
Brora, inland to Loch Brora, then up into the hills to emerge at
Rogart before turning left back and joining the main A9 at The
Mound, just north of the Fleet estuary crossing. The scenery is
stunning and peaceful. After you cross the Fleet I would also
recommend that you then again turn off the A9, this time to
the left, and take the road to Embo and Dornoch. Here you
pass along Loch Fleet where you can often see a pod of harbour
seals (there are I think many collective nouns for seals but I
rather like 'pod') basking in the sunshine on the sandbanks. It
is a beautiful sight in a beautiful spot.

A few miles south lies the delightful town of Dornoch and
many may be surprised that it is not my choice of course for this
next chapter. It is generally agreed that if Royal Dornoch were

situated within an hour of Edinburgh or Glasgow as opposed to an hour north of Inverness, it would be a regular venue for the Open Championship. It is a wonderful course and enjoys a setting as beautiful as Brora and would certainly qualify for this book in terms of overall experience. It also attracts many American visitors because it was the birthplace and home of a famous golf course designer, Donald Ross, who left for America in 1899 and became a well-known player, but more importantly a renowned golf course designer. A number of top American courses (current venues for the US Open such as Pinehurst, Oak Hill and Oakland Hills) were designed by him and it is possible to see features of Dornoch in many of these courses. The Donald Ross connection attracts many American visitors to Dornoch (you can even rent the cottage in the town where he was born). While Royal Dornoch is one of my favourite courses, it does not qualify for this book because it is in some ways too famous and too tough. In the summer it is generally booked-up with visitors (and so is expensive) and if you are anything above a mid to low handicapper you will find it very challenging unless the weather conditions are benign.

The other course we pass on the journey south is Skibo which also has a famous history and strong links to America. Skibo Castle is now a 'members only' hotel and the course is a part of it. The castle was originally a residence of the Bishop of Caithness. From the 16th to the 19th centuries it was in various private hands and after falling into disrepair was bought in the 1890s by Andrew Carnegie, the Scottish born industrialist who made his fortune in America. He retired to the castle and it remained in his family until 1982. The private members 'Carnegie Club' was founded in the 1990s by Peter de Savary and though the ownership has changed it remains that today. Considerable investment has gone into restoring the golf course as well and it enjoys a very pretty setting overlooking the Dornoch Firth.

But neither of these two great courses fit my criteria so instead I am headed for Tain where we find a famous distillery and a less famous golf course.

Tain is the oldest Royal Burgh in Scotland, being granted its Royal Charter by King Malcolm in 1066. Indeed the town has had an interesting history as a refuge for both Robert the Bruce and Bonnie Prince Charlie, and was even used as a location for D-Day landing exercises. The town's museum will tell you more. Today it is a small town of just 3,500 people. It does not attract as many visitors as Dornoch and as such has a less prosperous feel to it, but nonetheless there are a number of interesting old buildings.

There are actually two distilleries on the south side of the Dornoch Firth; Balblair, owned by a large Thai multi-national drinks group, is just west of the A9 at Edderton, but right on the main road at the turning to Tain is Glenmorangie, undoubtedly one of Scotland's most famous whisky brands. Let us start with its pronunciation, which many still get wrong. The emphasis should be on the second, as opposed to the third, syllable. If I had to choose a product for a newcomer to malt whisky to try I think Glenmorangie would be a strong contender. It is a very accessible taste; rich and sweet, maybe not as subtle as some malts but delightful all the same. The brand was one of the first famous malts.

It is worth explaining the definition of whisky in the UK, which has been legislated for many years, the most recent being the 'Scotch Whisky Regulations of 2009'. To be called Scotch whisky it has to be wholly matured in its cask in Scotland for a minimum of three years. There are effectively five types of whisky: single malt (whisky made with malted barley and coming from one distillery), single grain (the same but made with grain, which could be any grain but is likely to be wheat), blended malt and blended grain (malt and grain whisky from more than one distillery) and then blended scotch which is a mixture of malt and grain and is the most common type.

Malt whisky accounts for less than 10 per cent of total Scotch consumption, 90 per cent being blended Scotch. Single and blended grain whiskies are very rare. Most of the big distilleries, even ones producing some famous malt whisky brands, will sell the majority of their output for blending, as we saw at Clynelish where the majority of its production was for its leading premium blended brand, Johnnie Walker. While consumption of blended Scotch whisky is in decline, sales of malts are growing. And while Scotland is famous for whisky, nearly half of world whisky sales are of Indian whisky. Indeed, 8 of the world's top 10 whisky brands are in fact Indian; the only two others featuring in the top ten are Johnnie Walker (3rd) and Jack Daniels (6th). With a growing Asian population this is unlikely to change, though this growing and increasingly affluent population is what will fuel the market growth over the coming decades, as there is a clear correlation between the growth of a middle class and whisky consumption. So the future for the Scottish industry lies in premium malts; competing with locally produced standard product will be difficult. The other statistic which I find fascinating is that one country stands far ahead of all others on per capita consumption of whisky, behind the UK in third place and the US in second. Well, I would not have guessed that it is France. Whisky, on top of the pastis, wine and brandy! No wonder they shrug their shoulders.

So, with France being such an important market and famous Scottish malt whisky brands becoming valuable global assets, it is perhaps not a surprise that Glenmorangie is now owned by the French luxury brands company LVMH (Louis Vuitton, Moet, Hennessy).

Glenmorangie Barrel

LVMH has invested heavily in Glenmorangie. The distillery has a very plush visitor centre and shop and the buildings and site look immaculately smart and tidy. Even the car park has a quality feel to it. As you would expect from an international premium brands company, money has not been spared in design and marketing. The bottle was redesigned some years ago and is a very distinctive shape – some might say the French influence is obvious as it has more of the look of a brandy bottle rather than a whisky bottle. The marketers have also exploited the brand's heritage, incorporating the Pictish Cadboll Stone into the label design as a brand icon. It is a big distillery, the feature being the magnificent still room with its vaulted ceiling. They claim to have the tallest stills in Scotland (Glenkinchie say theirs are 'the largest'!) and they are certainly distinctive. Being over five metres tall (the same height as a fully grown adult giraffe) it is claimed they ensure only the purest vapours make it through distillation thereby delivering a smoother taste. Much is also spoken about their water source from the local Tarlogie Springs but there is much debate about whether the type of water, which is of course added early in the process, has any material impact on the end product. The one factor which everyone agrees does impact the final product is the maturation in casks. Here Glenmorangie also claims to be distinctive: they only ever use a cask twice and believe that they are pioneers in the art of maturation. Many of their special edition whiskies have experimented with different cask types, something which has become an increasing trend in other distilleries. Finally, the story of the original '16 men of Tain' who made the whisky, is very much part of the brand statement though they seem recently to have dropped the '16' and refer to them as just 'the Men of Tain', presumably as automation has led to a need for fewer than that to run the whole process. I also didn't see any 'Ladies of Tain' employees involved in the production process, though nowadays there are more people employed in providing the tours and in the shop than in the distillery itself and our tour guide, as at Clynelish, was a very knowledgeable lady. Whisky is more than just a product; it is a tourist and enthusiast experience.

The tour is professionally organised, starting with a video explaining the production process, and includes all of the production facilities including a visit to a warehouse. The warehousing is extensive and the one included in the tour is of the traditional 'dunnage' style – barrels laid out on the floor in a single story building. They also have more modern racked warehouses, though some believe that how the product is stored can affect the final product and the amount of product loss during maturation; the famous 'Angel's Share'. As ever it ends with a tasting (I should mention that to get the most out of distillery visits you should be accompanied by a driver!). My problem with these tastings is that they are rather out of context. It is like hitting a golf ball on a golf range. It just isn't the real thing. I think tasting whisky properly requires context, the right mood and the right time of day. Some of the distilleries will allow you to take your dram away with you and I think this is the best idea.

So Glenmorangie is an example of an old Scottish brand and product becoming a globally marketed brand asset. The visitor centre is part of the brand communication which emphasises its history and seeks to define its product distinctiveness through its tall stills and maturation policy.

Glenmorangie means 'Glen of Tranquillity' and tranquil is probably a more appropriate adjective for the setting of the golf course rather than the distillery which is next to the A9. Tain Golf Club is situated below the town, down on the estuary past the cemetery. As you enter the car park you are greeted by four statutes carved from old tree trunks, which in turn feature 'Tain',

'Golf' 'Club' and then the unmistakeable figure of Old Tom Morris. These were conifers which used to screen off the first tee and were cut down a few years ago, and instead of removing the trunks it was decided to get a local craftsman to make a feature out of them. Old Tom is in many ways the father of golf in Scotland. He won four of the first eight Open Championships. Originally from St Andrews, he was brought up, and learned his golf from, Allan Robertson, who was generally regarded as the world's first professional golfer (Robertson never played in The Open because he died before the first one was held). Morris was the son of a local weaver but under Robertson's tutelage became addicted to golf, caddying, greenkeeping and helping Robertson with his golf equipment business, much of which entailed making golf balls. In those days golf balls were called 'featheries', being made out of cow hide stuffed with goose down. It was this which caused Morris to break with Robertson. In the late 1840s a new type of ball emerged moulded from a rubbery substance called gutta-percha, derived from the sap of the Malaysian gutta tree. These balls soon became popular being both longer lasting and much cheaper to make than the old featheries. Other ball makers soon recognised the potential in these new balls but Allan Robertson, who clearly had the 'featherie' market in St Andrews to himself, tried to eschew this new technology. One day he found Morris experimenting with the new ball and immediately dismissed him. Morris, shocked at Roberston's emotional behaviour, was then lured to the great rival golf centre on the west coast, Prestwick, where, from 1851, he became greenkeeper, course designer and ran his own ball making business making the new gutta-percha balls. While at Prestwick he was involved in starting the Open

Championship, which was held at Prestwick from the inaugural event in 1860 until 1873 when St Andrews held the event for the first time. Indeed Morris struck the first shot in the first Open Championship, though he did not win it. Old Tom (he became 'Old Tom' when his son, 'Young Tom', became an even more successful golfer winning four consecutive Opens from 1868, before his life was cut tragically short – see Chapter 7) returned to St Andrews in 1864 (Robertson had died in 1859) and became a much sought-after course designer. Golf took off as a sport across not only Scotland but also England, Wales and particularly Ireland. We will come across his design both in the next chapter at Moray and later at Machrihanish, but among other famous creations were Westward Ho! in Devon and Lahinch on the west coast of Ireland. As courses developed many clubs wanted Old Tom to give design advice.

The course in some ways is not a traditional links as, at times, it routes quite far inland (though the land remains 'links') and you are surrounded by fields of sheep, something not usually associated with links courses. There are also, at the top end of the course, trees, which again are not normally a feature of links courses. It was first laid out by Old Tom in 1890 and is quite a gentle course. There are few dramatic changes in elevation, no gimmicks and arguably few really memorable holes. The exception is the Par 4 11th, appropriately named 'The Alps'. The fairways are quite generous and the greens flat rather than strongly undulating. The test comes from subtle changes in direction of the holes and therefore the wind (unlike Brora this is not an 'out and back' course) as well as the appearance of the Tain river at the 2nd and 17th. On 'The Alps' the drive is from a lofted tee to a fairway which, rather unlike the others, is undulating rather than flat, and narrower than most. For the second shot you are confronted with three large hillocks, the central one having a small red and white post on it. Beyond the hillocks lies the green which nestles just above the beach. It is perhaps reminiscent of the 14th at North Berwick as the second shot is blind and has only just to carry the hillocks to reach the green. It is a good hole though perhaps technically not the best.

This begs the question; what makes a hole a good one? What constitutes 'a good hole'? Often, after playing a particular hole on a course I haven't played before, I will say; 'That was a good hole'. Sometimes I will stand on the tee and say this 'looks a good hole' even before I have played it. There are no strict rules. I think the 'look' of a hole on the tee is important. It should display before you what the challenge is. A good hole will normally have a shape to it, but that doesn't mean that you can't have a good straight hole. Some dog-leg holes are in my view good but some also not so good. It is difficult to articulate but let me try.

There are a number of features that might make a good hole. An element of risk versus reward can be good. By taking a particular driving line (perhaps close to a bunker) you can be rewarded with an easier second shot, whereby a safer line will make the second shot longer or more difficult. Of course many modern courses use risk and reward with lots of water. I am not a fan of this, partly because it is often contrived and also the punishment can be too much. A ball that hits a green and then perhaps rolls back just into the water is effectively giving a two shot penalty. In my view the punishment is too harsh. Bunkers are usually only a one shot penalty and there remains the opportunity to recover. I am in favour of more subtle risk and reward.

I think the look of a hole is very important and so some 'shape' or change in elevation is generally necessary. An element of optical illusion can also be good and was often used by the greatest course designers. Placing bunkers not just up against a green but say 20 yards short is a good example. The design of the green is also important. It should have some form of protection and should sit in a natural looking setting.

Like many things, what is a good hole to one person is not to others. Some people I know don't like blind holes (like 'The Alps') saying that they are unfair (I suggest that they don't bother visiting The Machrie, our last course!). I think that holes with blind shots can be good. I don't think blind shots themselves are bad; there are good and bad ones. There is the famous blind Par 3 at Cruden Bay in Aberdeenshire which rather divides opinion. Anstruther, in Fife, has a small 9 hole course which claims to have the world's only 'dog-leg par 3', the aptly name 'Rockies', where you aim high over the side of a rocky ridge to an unseen green.

It is worth reading what some of the great designers thought themselves. The designer who I think has the best attitude is Alister Mackenzie (he will feature at Blairgowrie in Chapter 5). He was an advocate of golf being first and foremost a source of enjoyment, so to him the ideal hole was *'one that affords the greatest pleasure to the greatest number, gives the fullest advantage to accurate play, stimulates players to improve their game, and never becomes monotonous.'*

So while 'The Alps' may be the most memorable hole, it is probably not the best. The second deserves a mention; a gentle dog leg Par 4 with the second shot over the river to a plateau green. I have to declare an interest here – I birdied it when I last played it (since you ask, a good drive, a seven iron and 20 foot putt). It is amazing when discussing good holes with golfing colleagues how strong the correlation is between their preference expressed for a particular hole and how successful they have been in playing it. The same is true of favourite golf courses. Ultimately it has to be said that there aren't good and bad holes; it is a personal thing. Indeed, what makes a good malt whisky? I don't particularly like strong peaty malts; I prefer milder ones. That doesn't make peaty whiskies bad and milder ones good. I like short Par 4 holes and dislike what I see as contrived water hazards. The definition of a good hole is the same as that of a good malt whisky – it is what you like. And indeed what you like some days may not be what you like another.

The green on 'The Alps', the 11th, is the first time that you encounter the sea and the views across the Dornoch Firth to Dornoch itself and then up the coast to Golspie and Brora are delightful. The next two holes are on this same piece of land by the sea but are more conventional. The 13th is a long par 5 which heads back to a green framed by a line of trees in the distance, giving it a very appealing look.

At 16 and 17, Tain shares with Golspie the distinction of two consecutive Par 3s; the first, relatively short playing down over the river and the second playing much longer and flatter, again over the river which comes uncomfortably close to the green on the right. The 18th then returns to the clubhouse with a fairly gentle Par 4.

Tain is a very pleasant course in very pleasant surroundings. It is a shame that it misses out on many of the visitors who make the pilgrimage to Dornoch. It is a marvellous golfing experience and exceptional value – take a look at its website where there is a helicopter video of every hole and you will be immediately tempted. It is beginning to market itself. There is the Dornoch Firth Pass which gives you a 30 per cent discount off the Dornoch courses, Brora, Golspie and Tain. When I visited Tain, the Secretary was over in Holland on a mission to drum up Dutch visitors. Courses such as Tain need visitors to sustain them and for the majority of mid-handicap golfers are actually much more suitable than Dornoch. It is also a very real local club; the clubhouse is not plush but very welcoming, and contains a lot of Old Tom Morris memorabilia. It is a very rewarding visit.

Tain therefore delivers two different examples of whisky and golf – a big brand classic in Glenmorangie and a much lower profile and modest (in a positive sense), yet rewarding, golf club. I am beginning to recognise a significant difference between my golfing and whisky experiences; an expert whisky enthusiast may favour the less well known distilleries while the expert golfer may want only to play the famous courses. I will see if that theory holds.

The Clubhouse at Moray

Moray's clubhouse is one of my favourites in the whole of
Scotland. It is not only perfectly situated overlooking the
course and the coastline but is architecturally both pleasing
and interesting, while inside the welcome is always warm.

A 'Butt', a 'Hogshead' and a 'Barrel' at Benromach

The barrel is the most commonly used size (190-200 litres), generally ex-bourbon barrels made of American white oak. Hogsheads are slightly larger (225-250 litres), are also usually made from American white oak, and are often used for longer maturation periods. Butts are much bigger (up to 500 litres) and are often ex- sherry casks made from Spanish oak.

CHAPTER THREE

Moray

'Golf is an indispensable adjunct to high civilisation'

Andrew Carnegie (1835-1919)
Scottish/American industrialist and philanthropist

 IT IS LESS than an hour's drive south from Tain, down the A9 across the famous 'Black Isle' (not actually an island, but a peninsula with charming countryside) to Inverness, where a fine new bridge crosses the Moray Firth. The Moray Firth has a delightful stretch of north-facing coastline from Inverness all the way to Fraserburgh, by which time it has long since stopped being a firth. There is much to see along this coast from Fort George, the old home of the Black Watch, to the pretty resort town of Nairn, two important RAF bases at Kinloss and Lossiemouth, Gordounstoun School where the Prince of Wales was educated, and attractive coastal and fishing towns and villages, such as Portsoy and Cullen (home of the eponymous 'skink', a delicious smoked haddock soup).

Today the two most famous courses are probably Nairn and Castle Stuart. Nairn is an old established club in a small resort town, a top class course which hosted the 1992 Walker Cup as well as many other amateur tournaments. Castle Stuart is one of the best new links courses built in the UK and has hosted the Scottish Open on several occasions. It is the work of Mark Parsinen, an American who has become a passionate advocate of the greatness of traditional Scottish links courses, and in Kingsbarns near St Andrews, and Castle Stuart has created their modern equivalent. But the club I have chosen is the appropriately named Moray and is, in my view, much under-rated and certainly has all the characteristics of a classic Scottish links club.

For whisky there is plenty of choice locally around Elgin while it would even be possible to partner it with one of the numerous Speyside distilleries which are not far away. But again I have chosen a less well-known name, Benromach, a small distillery which had been closed but which a few years ago was re-opened and has been restored to its former glory.

The whisky industry is facing exciting times. Not only are the big companies like Diageo, Pernod Ricard and LMVH investing in growth, but private independent distillers are seeing opportunities. New distilleries are being opened and old distilleries are being re-opened. In Fife we will see an example of the former while Benromach is an example of the latter.

The Benromach distillery dates back to 1898 and was in various ownerships during the first part of the century. It was mothballed during the major industry downturn of the 1930s before being re-opened in 1937 and eventually ending up in the Distillers company portfolio in 1953. The distillery was refurbished by Distillers in the 1960s but was once again mothballed in 1983 as part of a rationalisation programme in response to industry over-capacity. It was then bought, ten years later, by Gordon and Macphail, a well-known family independent whisky bottler. The business started as a family partnership in

Elgin in 1895 and while it became a limited company in the 1970s, it is still owned and run by the 3rd and 4th generation of the original Urquhart family who set it up. As well as buying newly-made spirit from distilleries all over Scotland and maturing it themselves to produce ranges of specialist whiskies, the business runs a famous retail store in Elgin which, as well as selling whisky, now offers a range of premium foods.

The business had survived for nearly a century as an independent bottler of spirit from a number of top Scottish distilleries. Gordon and MacPhail then marketed them under a range of 'brands'; Private Collection, Connoisseurs Choice etc. The business is totally sustainable as most of its assets are its valuable stocks of maturing spirit, some of which are very old, very rare and therefore very valuable. In 2015 they released a 75 year old Mortlach, allegedly the oldest malt ever bottled. Only 75 bottles were made available and would have cost tens of thousands of pounds. One of their advertising slogans is 'the wood makes the whisky' reflecting their focus on maturation as opposed to distilling.

The decision to buy a distillery and become a whisky producer was therefore a major departure for the business. The distillery comprised only the buildings, as United Distillers (as it was then – now it is Diageo) kept the stock and removed the equipment so they were starting from scratch. Their goal was to reproduce a traditional, lightly-peated, Speyside malt which they felt (and as an independent bottler, they were in a position to observe) had lost its distinctive character since the 1960s. To do this they decided to keep the scale small and the level of automation minimal. It took them five years to start production after installing a copper domed mash tun, four larch washbacks and a pair of copper pot stills. The official opening was made by HRH Prince Charles in 1998. The process is traditional with no gauges relying, as they state, on 'touch, feel, sound and sight' from what they call 'their fourth ingredient'; the three still men who operate the process. There is demonstrably a pride and a passion for their process and the product that results.

So what is it at Benromach that makes their product distinctive? They claim to be the only distillery that uses a mix of brewers' and distillers' yeast, and unlike Glenmorangie who only use first and second fill casks, at Benromach they will only use first fill casks – a mixture of sherry and bourbon. They also believe that the storage conditions are important and they use dunnage-style warehouses which produce the right level of humidity.

It is difficult to challenge their credentials. While the single malt market is in many ways quite young, pioneered by Glenfiddich and Glenmorangie in the 1960s, Gordon and McPhail had effectively been producing single malts since the turn of the century, albeit using spirit from a range of distilleries. While they controlled the maturation, probably the single biggest differentiation factor, as they were not a producer they did not control the spirit making process. Their move into distilling as well as maturation gave them control over the whole process for their Benromach brand. In effect they are admitting that while the maturation is the most important factor, the quality of spirit is also relevant. The standard 10-year-old Benromach, they describe as fruity, sweet, with a hint of chocolate and a touch of smokiness. They also, using their maturation experience, produce special editions with finishing (maybe the final two years of maturation) in specific wine casks. My personal favourite in their range is in fact their Organic malt, which when it was launched was an industry first, being matured in virgin oak casks. This probably reflects my preference for milder, fresh tasting whiskies.

A Larch Washback

The Benromach site is not in the most scenic location, being on a small industrial estate on the south side of the pleasant town of Forres some ten miles east of Elgin. The buildings, however, are typical late Victorian and have been well restored. There is a small visitor centre from where tours are given by passionate employees who are strong advocates of the Gordon and McPhail story. You can sense that this is a family business. Whether the distillery makes money is debateable; it is, however, very much part of the family business proposition. The tasting is very informal and informative as they give you examples of different peat levels, and also the organic, and seek your opinions. They also give you little bottles to take away in case you are driving. The shop in nearby Elgin is well worth a visit, an impressive old Victorian building near the centre of town which, as well as containing a whisky shop, is a sort of North of Scotland equivalent of Fortnum and Masons or the Harrods or Selfridges Food Halls, selling a range of premium food and drinks. Also worth a visit, situated in lovely rural surroundings on the south-west side of Forres, is the now closed Dallas Dhu distillery. This was also mothballed in 1983 by Distillers, but unlike Benromach all the original equipment remained intact and it was sold to Historic Scotland three years later to become a museum. It is an excellent way of understanding the whisky-making progress and seeing how the industry developed. There is also still a small amount of stock of Dallas Dhu whisky and occasional rare bottlings, the latest being by Gordon and McPhail.

Having visited the Diageo distillery at Clynelish and the French owned Glenmorangie, it is encouraging to see a small independent Scottish business still flourishing and continuing to play a very distinctive role in the market. It remains a proud family business and won two Queen's Awards for Enterprise in 2009 and 2013. I am beginning also to learn more about what makes one whisky different from another. Clearly the maturation is the biggest factor but it cannot be the only one or why would Gordon and MacPhail have moved into distilling? The mystery remains to me; once the spirit is made how much of the end product characteristics are set?

Moray Golf Club is also distinctive in its own way. It has two splendid links courses, the old designed again by Old Tom and the new by Henry Cotton, the best British golfer of the 1930s. Yes, this is the third course in the book and it is yet another links. It is time to say why I enjoy links golf so much and, along with others, believe it is the purest form of golf. To many it is seen as too random, too unfair. Often a good shot will not produce the desired result if it bounces just a few inches away from a perfect shot. Some people complain that too many good shots are not rewarded; there is too much 'bad luck'. What is strange is that these golfers generally only talk of their bad luck during a round and rarely mention the good luck they will inevitably have had. The ball that kicks fortuitously in towards the pin is generally banked as a good shot as opposed to a bit of good fortune!

Tom Watson, the American five-times Open Champion, in his forward to the book *True Links*, talks about how he at first was suspicious of links golf. Like many Americans he searched for certainty; a 160 yard shot is an 8 iron and depending on the shot will either hop forward a little or spin backwards. On a links course, 160 yards could be anything from a wedge to a 4 iron, depending on the wind and the lie of the land. The same shot played with a wedge in the morning could be a 4 iron in the afternoon. That is what is so great about links golf; it requires thinking, not just mechanical calculation. Often too, there are several options as to how to play the shot; a low runner or high in the air; or play safe, away from the pin and take out the uncertainty of some humps and bumps in case you get some 'bad luck'! To me it is definitely the purest form of golf.

And there is no one better than Tom Watson to extol the virtues of links golf because if anyone has the right to complain about bad luck it is he. At the grand old age of 59 he was leading The Open and needed just a Par 4 at the 18th hole at Turnberry in 2009 to win. He played a perfect drive to the centre of the fairway. He then played what he thought was a perfect 8 iron which landed just on the front of the green but took a hard bounce and ran through and over the back of the green from where he failed to get up and down in two. He went on to lose to Stewart Cink in the play-off.

He got an unlucky bounce. It was unfair. He played a good shot and was unduly punished. He will not see it like that. It is true that the ball might, a few inches away, have bounced more softly and stayed on the green. But by landing it where he did there was always a chance it could run through the back. It was probably the right shot if he needed to get near the pin. But he needed a 4 and not a 3. Maybe he should have calculated that and played a little more conservatively and taken that possibility out of the equation. He admitted also that perhaps a bit of adrenalin in his body made him hit it just a little harder than he had intended. Maybe he should have adjusted for that. Like life, golf, and particularly links golf, is full of 'ifs' and 'buts'; that is its beauty.

So I do regard links golf as the purest form of the game. However, many great courses have 'linkslike' characteristics. 'Heathland' courses are often the inland equivalent of proper links courses (the two featured in this book are good examples). It is perhaps no accident that there are no 'parkland' courses on my list. It is not that I have any aversion to parkland courses – indeed I am a member of one, though admittedly it is a very old parkland course. I suppose the comparison can be made with blended whisky as opposed to single malts. There is a role for both and there are some very good and enjoyable blends which have similar characteristics but the purest form of the product is undoubtedly the single malt.

One of the features of the Moray Club is its clubhouse. I think the clubhouse is very much part of the experience and it has been a significant factor in my choosing of the nine courses which, with two exceptions, all have clubhouses of character. It is again difficult to define what the perfect clubhouse is but there are in my view a number of factors: Does it have a good view of the course? Is it architecturally pleasing? Is it welcoming to visitors? When you walk into it, is there a sense of history? I enjoy wandering around old clubhouses and looking at the memorabilia on display and in particular the trophy cabinet, where often there is a remarkable array of silverware of various shapes and sizes.

Clubhouses are also important because that is where you have lunch. And lunch is often an important aspect of golf. Golf is not just about the 18 holes outside and how you played. It is the sport, the competition but also the companionship which will often include time spent in the clubhouse either having a drink or having lunch. Some clubs take lunch very seriously, others not so. Some do it well, others not so well. There are different types of lunch from, at one extreme, Prestwick, for example, where for a formal lunch you must wear a jacket and tie and go into the dining room and sit, next in line, at a big table alongside other golfers and you are served a four course meal. The food is honest fare as opposed to fine cuisine but honest fare is what golf requires. Most clubs will serve lunches at the bar. The food is seldom complicated; soup, sandwiches, burgers and fish and chips. When done right, it can make such a big difference to the overall golfing experience. The best are those that don't try to do too much – a limited choice of homemade soup, good bread, good quality fresh fish and chips and freshly made sandwiches will satisfy most. Clubs looking to attract visitors or even new members should pay attention to this aspect.

The clubhouse at Moray is my favourite on this tour. The great course designer Harry Colt, who I will cover later in the book, saw the siting of the clubhouse as part of the design of a course and always 'favoured a fine view from the clubhouse windows'. The clubhouse at Moray delivers comprehensively on this, occupying the perfect position, high above the course, giving a magnificent view over both courses and the coastline. You can watch spectacular sunsets from the bar window. It is also a handsome looking building while inside it is practical rather than luxurious and in this sense very real and down-to-earth. There are the normal trophy cabinets and a sense that it is a local amenity – I am sure that members also go there when they are not playing golf. The food is simple but good.

I last visited Moray on a Sunday in April. There was a monthly medal on the Old (the main course) in the morning, but I asked if I could play the New and then play the Old later in the day when the medal was finished. The Professional was very relaxed; that would be fine and I paid a green fee for the Old while he said I could just go and play the New. This makes the New sound like just a practice course but it is in fact much better than that. There was an original second 9 holes, like at many courses, and in 1979 Henry Cotton transformed it into 18. It is a gentle course, not long, but very tight. The greens are quite friendly being fairly flat but there is a premium on accuracy because there is plenty gorse to catch any wayward shots.

The course starts rather awkwardly as you have to walk down the first of the Old to reach the first tee on the New, which is behind the first green of the Old. It then wends its way between holes on the Old before finding its own piece of land over the other side of a burn towards the lighthouse. The best three holes are 9, 10 and 11 which are the only ones by the sea. Both 9 and 10 require you to hit over the burn and are classic seaside links holes, while 11 is a short Par 3 facing directly inland. From 15 onwards the course again twists its way around the Old and the 18th green is next to the 18th tee on the Old. Off the yellow tees there are no Par 5s and the Par is just 68; off the Whites there are two and the course just extends beyond 6,000 yards. But length is not the point; the challenge here is to keep it straight and away from the gorse.

The Old, off the yellow tees, is also just a Par 68, having just one Par 5 and only three par 3s, and extends to 6,228 yards. The white tees only add 250 yards and a second par 5. It was designed by Old Tom Morris and opened in 1889, so belongs to the same era as Brora and Tain. The course is longer than the New though probably wider but has more character; the greens are less flat and have been located in natural positions (Henry Cotton clearly had much less choice nearly 80 years later). There are also many more memorable holes; the second playing to a hidden green close to a road; the long Par 3 4th; two interesting short Par 4s at 9 and 10 and then the best stretch by the sea, 15, a tricky Par 3, 16, a dog-leg Par 4 and then 17, a sweeping Par 5. Perhaps the best hole on the course, however, is the 18th which is very often not the case on a traditional 'out and back' Scottish links, where so often the final hole is designed simply to take the golfer back to the clubhouse. The 18th at Moray

Old does just this, but because of the clubhouse's impressive location, perched on a hill, the hole is a magnificent challenge. The drive is into a narrow but gathering humpy fairway from where the second shot requires you to hit up towards the green (generally not from a flat lie) which sits half way up the hill in front of the clubhouse. In truth the green is quite generous, but somehow the shot is very daunting and missing it either side gives problems. It is definitely the best 18th hole of my nine chosen courses and I know of few better.

There is one thing about Moray which has to be mentioned. The location is beautiful on the Moray Firth but at times it is not peaceful as the course neighbours RAF Lossiemouth, a major strategic UK air force base famous for being a base for Tornado and now Typhoon aircraft. When I visited recently on a Sunday there was no aircraft activity, but I remember on my previous visit a pair of earplugs would have been useful. The course actually houses landing lights on the 13th and 14th fairways for the runway which require a local rule – they are deemed 'temporary immovable obstructions'.

Benromach and Moray offer the best of true Scottishness; their beginnings were within ten years of each other and they have both stayed true to their Scottish origins. Both are authentic examples of the best quality that Scotland can offer, every bit as good a golfing or whisky-drinking experience as more internationally renowned courses or brands.

Boat of Garten Golf Club; 3rd hole

This is perhaps not the most dramatic view of Boat of Garten because
it misses the imposing backdrop of the Cairngorms which is such a
feature of the course environment but it does typify the heathland feel
of the course. As everywhere on a golf course, the colours will again
vary dramatically with the seasons with heather a particular feature.
This is April just before the leaves start to appear on the trees but still
there is colour and texture everywhere such is the variety of vegetation.

Carrbridge on Speyside

The Carrbridge packhorse bridge, the oldest known stone bridge in the Highlands, was built in 1716. The bridge was built to enable access for funeral processions to Duthil church when the River Dulnain was in full spate. The original parapets were washed away in a major flood in 1829 leaving the central arch giving it such an unusual appearance.

CHAPTER FOUR

Speyside

Whisky 'Being moderately taken it cuttethvfleume, it lighteneth the mynd, it quickeneth the spirits, it cureth the hydropsie, it pounceth the stone, it repelleth gravel, it puffeth away ventositie, it kepyth and preserveth the eyes drom dazelying, the tongue from lispying, the teeth from chatterying, the throte from rattlying, the weasand from stieflying, the stomach from womblying, the harte from swellying, the bellie from writhing, the giuts from rumblying, the hands from shivering, the sinews from shrinkying, the veynes from crumplying, the bones from akying, the marrow from soakying, and truly it is the sovereign liquor if it be orderlie taken'

Raphael Holinshed (1529-1580)

English Chronicler

BENROMACH IS ACTUALLY is classified as a 'Speyside' malt though it is some 30 miles as the crow flies from the River Spey and the location is very much part of the Moray Firth rather than Speyside itself. The main Speyside area is an approximately 40 mile stretch of the A95 from Aviemore on the A9 in the west up to Aberlour and Craigellachie and onto Dufftown on the A941. It is an area of great beauty but also quite different from what we have so far experienced. The valley is framed by the dramatic Cairngorms in the southern part which give way to slightly more gentle scenery at the north end. The place names also have a considerable romance about them; Ballindalloch, Knockando, Archiestown, Craigellachie, Dufftown. The southern end, near the A9, is the most developed, with Aviemore probably Scotland's premier ski resort and now quite developed for the summer holiday season. Aviemore no longer feels quintessentially Scottish. Aberlour and Dufftown, however, at the north end of the region, remain just that.

Speyside presents something of a dilemma. Choosing just one distillery seems to do the region an injustice as it accounts for over 60 per cent of the industry's capacity. But to choose two would mean I would need to feature two golf courses and in truth that would mean leaving out another worthier candidate. I considered Dufftown, which is one of Scotland's highest courses and has some dramatic views. It has some good holes with its famous 10th, a 467 yard Par 4, with an elevation drop from tee to green of over 300 feet! For a green fee of just £20 it is very much worth a visit, though in truth is not really a classic Scottish course. The next strongest candidate was Granton-on-Spey which is set in a pretty location within the town and has at least nine great holes amidst delightful pine forests. However, the course I have chosen, Boat of Garten, has, in my view, 18 great holes and is definitely worthy of its entry, being an example of a classic inland course and importantly also very beautiful (I would suggest that it is not possible to have a 'classic' course that isn't also 'beautiful' as beauty would be one of my criteria for being classic.)

I then spent a lot of time considering which distillery to feature. Glenfiddich, probably the original single malt and the oldest privately owned whisky brand, was a strong candidate.

Its distillery, situated in Dufftown, is also very charming. What about The Macallan, another world famous brand and a distinctively produced product and a very smart distillery? Or Glenfarclas or Craigellachie or... there are too many options.

I ended up with Glenlivet. Some might call it an uninspiring choice but it has a number of interesting characteristics, owned by Pernod Ricard (a further clue here perhaps about the French's predilection for whisky), it is America's favourite malt whisky brand and its distillery is situated in an immensely beautiful location.

James Braid

A surprising feature of the market for 'single malts' is how recent it is. It was probably Glenfiddich and Glenmorangie which were the forerunners of today's highly diversified market. Glenfiddich was launched as a 'straight malt' in 1961 and Glenmorangie followed. While many of the distilleries have long histories, for much of that history they have been producing whisky for blending and indeed product for blending still accounts for the vast majority of production. It is worth considering some statistics. Less than 10 per cent of the whisky produced in Scotland is single malt, but this has grown from less than 1 per cent in the 1970s. Of course these trends are complicated by the product. In the early days of the growth of malt whisky, as the market potential was being recognised, the view was that the product had to be accompanied by an 'age statement', namely at least five years and increasingly ten years aged. Obviously there is a considerable lead-time associated with production being able to respond to the marketers' requirements. Ten and twelve year olds have of late become the norm, but with the growth in the market the producers now have a problem. They can't just produce endless quantities of ten- year-olds as this would need to have been planned ten years ago! So today you will increasingly find 'non-age dominated' malts with fancy marketing names. Effectively these are younger whiskies given a specific character either by blending different aged barrels or using different woods for maturation, either throughout or in the finishing. An age statement can only relate to the youngest spirit used in any single malt; so a whisky made from a blend of five-year-old spirit with some twelve-year-old matured spirit can only be called a five-year- old.

Glenlivet is situated on the Glenlivet estate south of the river Spey. It is an area where whisky has been distilled for many centuries and the story of Glenlivet is in many ways the story of the Scottish whisky industry. It had been a cottage industry in this area of Speyside, as well as across the Highlands, for hundreds of years, but gradually during the 17th and 18th centuries taxation had increased to the extent that distilling became illicit rather than legitimate. During the 1790s, with the government looking to increase the tax take to fund the Napoleonic Wars, taxation was increased further (governments then, as today, assumed that increasing taxes generates more tax income when evidence generally shows that the opposite to be the case). This drove a number of the lowland distilleries out of business (that is why higher taxes don't bring more tax income!) but Glenlivet was helped by its remoteness from Edinburgh, which enabled the distillers to carry on their illicit trade hidden from the excise men. It was the Duke of Gordon who helped lobby Parliament, pointing out the self-defeating nature of the ever increasing level of duty. The result was the 1823 Excise Act which reduced the level and also the minimum capacity of stills thereby allowing the smaller producers to operate legally and prosper. It was George Smith who in 1824 became the first Glenlivet distiller to operate legally, obtaining his licence in November 1824 and building a new distillery at Upper Drumin. There were still financial difficulties in the early years, and Smith was indebted to the Duke for a loan to keep the distillery going. By 1830 it had reached an output of 500 gallons a week. By 1859 a new distillery had been built nearby at Minmore and output reached 4,000 gallons a week, and the opening of the railway station at Ballindalloch just five miles away revolutionised the distribution and therefore the sales potential. George's son, John Gordon, was now running the business and it was he who registered the trademark Glenlivet. However, the railway had also proved a boost for other local distillers who looked also to trade under the reputation of the Glenlivet name. A legal battle ensued which ended in a compromise whereby other local distilleries were able to add 'Glenlivet' as a suffix to their distillery name while only Smith was able to call his whisky 'The Glenlivet' is how the brand name of today was born.

The 20th century saw periods of boom and bust for the industry. Heavy production in the late 19th century had caused a glut which brought about the closure of many distilleries in the early years of the 20th century. This was followed by the war, which inevitably had a serious effect, forcing most distilleries to close. After the war demand returned and production volumes rose with exports to the United States and the Empire, but then the industry was again hit by both Prohibition in America and the Great Depression. The Glenlivet was one of only few malt whisky distilleries left working in Scotland in the early 1930s. The business was still in the original family being run by Bill Smith Grant, who had taken over responsibility after the Great War. It was he who saw the opportunity in America for a premium product, travelling there in 1934, and sales grew again substantially up until the outbreak of World War II. Again production had to cease during the war, as crops were transferred to wheat for bread production. However, after the war, demand yet again returned, especially in America, and The Glenlivet joined forces with Glen Grant in 1952. This new business saw sales grow and significant investment in the distilling process to meet demand. From 1970 onwards, as with many industries, it becomes a tale of mergers and acquisitions; first the business merged with two Edinburgh businesses and then, in 1978, The Glenlivet's Canadian distributor Seagram, which had already acquired both the Chivas Brothers and Strathisla distilleries, bought a controlling interest. Seagram oversaw significant global growth for the brand not only in North America but also in the Far East and Australasia. Then in the late 1990s ownership changed again, with Seagram selling The Glenlivet to the global French wine and spirits company Pernod Ricard, recognition that The Glenlivet, from its small beginnings as an illicit farm distillery, had grown into a global business and brand asset.

Pernod Ricard has certainly invested strongly in the business, with the distillery being one of the biggest and most impressive in Scotland. The business is set on becoming the world's biggest single malt and is now a close second to Glenfiddich, selling some 12 million bottles in 2013. It has become the biggest selling malt not only in the US but also in India. While the flagship product is a 12-year- old there are a number of older bottlings, as well as a more recent un-chill-filtered range called *Nadurra*. Some of these are marketed for the Duty Free market, while this range also includes different cask maturings such as sherry. The 12-year-old is, like Glenmorangie, a very accessible product; smooth, not heavily peated, and with a touch of sweetness. It does have a mass-produced feel about it or is that merely a result of seeing the highly automated process and the shiny stainless steel equipment and the more formal tasting? There could not be a more dramatic contrast between this and Benromach. I am increasingly of the view that the taste of the whisky is heavily influenced by the context of where and when you drink it.

The distillery itself is situated in a beautiful, quite remote, setting in Glenlivet and the site has been set up to cater for visitors, with a big visitor centre and frequent tours. The buildings themselves, however, are functional rather than aesthetically pleasing. It is perhaps a little too corporate and slick compared with some of the more intimate distilleries, but it represents the elite end of the industry; a global drinks business which has acquired a famous Scottish asset and is marketing it professionally. Somehow though, despite the beauty of the setting and the impressive equipment, it lacks the charm of Benromach.

While The Glenlivet is a 'Speyside' malt, the distillery itself is not that near the River Spey. It is actually situated between the rivers Livet and Avon, the former joining the latter, which is a tributary of the Spey, flowing northwards to join the Spey at Cragganmore. If you are visiting the area it is essential to drive along the A95, following the Spey from the A9 in the east up to probably the two most famous whisky towns of Aberlour and Dufftown. On this journey you will pass many of the most famous names in Scottish malts; Cragganmore, Cardhu, Knockando, Aberlour, The Balvenie, Glenfiddich, The Macallan, Glenfarclas, Mortlach. Also worth visiting is The Speyside Cooperidge, the largest independent cooperage (makers of whisky barrels) in the UK, which is preserving an historic art. Interestingly this business was sold in 2008 to a family-owned French business.

As I have said, the Speyside area is very beautiful and there is no more beautiful place within it than Boat of Garten which lies at the eastern end only a few miles off the A9. The name Boat of Garten derives from an ancient ferry crossing over the Spey in an area called 'garten', which comprised several villages and hamlets. Today's village is relatively new and grew up following the arrival of the railway in Victorian times. It has remained quite small with one hotel, two or three guest houses or bed and breakfast establishments, a very good restaurant and the Boat of Garten Golf and Tennis Club, which is probably the village's most vibrant community facility. There is, however, much else to do in the area, from fishing on the Spey to walking in the Cairngorms or the delightful woods around Loch Garten. Boat of Garten is also known as 'the osprey village' and a visit to the RSPB Osprey Centre is well worth it, whether you are a bird lover or not. Loch Garten is spectacularly beautiful, surrounded by dense birch woods, so you can understand why the ospreys, when they decided to return to Scotland to breed, chose this area. For bird enthusiasts there are other rare species as well including capercaillie, crested tits and goldeneye. Alternatively just walk around the delightfully peaceful loch, admire its beauty and wonder at the extraordinary amount of lichen on the trees, testament to the pureness of the air.

The first golf was played at Boat of Garten in 1898 when there were just six holes; rather bizarrely, two further holes were added in 1910, so from then until the 1930s it was an eight hole golf course. The tennis courts were built in 1921 but it wasn't until 1930 that additional land became available for rent and James Braid designed today's 18 hole course. There have been a few additions and modifications since but essentially the layout and style is that of Braid.

Boat of Garten is our first inland course, but in style it has many 'linksy' characteristics with, in summer at least, fast running bumpy fairways. It is a 'heathland' course very similar in style to some of the famous Surrey courses such as St George's Hill, The Berkshire and Sunningdale. It is not a long course at under 6,600 yards, with only one Par 4 over 400 yards (the 18th) and just two Par 5s. The emphasis here is on accuracy as the course wends its way through forests of lichen-encrusted silver birches with fairways lined with heather and patches of gorse and broom. The extent of lichen on the trees here too has to be seen to be believed. The fairways are at times quite narrow and while the bunkering is light, the greens are quite small. There are constant changes in elevation, relatively gentle at first but increasing as the round develops, which gives a big premium to club selection. A bit like the wind on a links course, the elevation can make a huge difference to the club required, especially if the fairways are dry – the difference between a downhill 150 yards and an uphill shot of the same distance could be up to three clubs.

The first hole is, unusually, a Par 3. It is fairly straightforward, 170 yards from the yellow tee boxes and 190 from the white ones with perhaps its most interesting feature being its enigmatic name, 'John's View'. I had to ask why at the clubhouse. It turns out that John Grant was the Club Professional and Greenkeeper (traditionally these were one and the same at many clubs in Scotland) for twenty years between 1951 and 1971. A well-known local figure and much loved servant to the club, the first hole, which had been, rather blandly, called 'fairview' was renamed in his memory. The practice of naming each hole on a course is not a peculiarly Scottish phenomenon but it is certainly more prevalent in Scotland than elsewhere. Very few of the major English courses do it, while in Ireland, for example, Royal Portrush does but Royal County Down does not. I find it charming as it adds character to the course. It stems probably from the Old Course at St Andrews, which not only names every hole but most of the bunkers too. I also love the different types of names used on courses: some will simply describe the hole; 'Long' or 'Short' or 'Home' for the finishing hole. The 18th at Boat of Garten is called 'Road' for no apparent reason though perhaps its shape is similar to its more famous namesake, the 17th at St Andrews, where a road is an obvious feature. Local landmarks are obviously popular; the 11th at Moray Old is called 'lighthouse' and the 13th here at Boat of Garten is called 'Spey'. I like the more intriguing names; the 4th on the Old Course at St Andrews is called 'ginger beer' which is less obvious than the 16th which is called 'corner of the dyke'! Famous golfers sometimes get holes named after them; at Carnoustie the difficult 6th is called 'Hogan's Alley', a reminder of Ben Hogan's devastatingly accurate play during his Open triumph in 1953 (in his only ever Open appearance) while Old Tom is probably the most featured name; with the 10th at old Moray and the 18th at St Andrews being examples. There are also some interesting conventions relating to topographical features; a hole with a big open fairway will be called 'the Elysian Fields' (Prestwick and St Andrews) or ones with large bunkers will be called 'Sahara' (Brora and Golspie are examples). The 9th at Tain is less specific, just called 'desert'. Holes with big dunes or hills will be called 'Alps' (Tain and Prestwick) or Himalayas (Prestwick). Perhaps my favourite though is the famous 14th hole at Dornoch which is simply called 'Foxy' – if you play it you will know why. I think the best naming strategy is a mixture of all these approaches; some descriptive, some recognising local landmarks and preferably some whimsical. Golf, like most aspects of life, is always enhanced by a touch of whimsy. Here the bunkers at St Andrews win; the 'beardies', the 'coffins', the 'spectacles', the 'principal's nose', 'hell bunker'; all wonderfully evocative names.

So back to Boat of Garten and the first hole, John's View, is a kind and modest start to the round. From the 2nd, a 350 yard

Par 4 with a slight dog-leg and a gentle rise to a raised green surrounded by silver birches, the true nature of the course appears. After another Par 3 at the third, the 4th is a long Par 5 with a delightfully bumpy fairway which again rises gently uphill. The 5th sees a more dramatic rise to the green but it is the 7th which delivers the most severe uphill slope, where the fairway climbs to a blind summit with the green nestled behind. Holes 8, 9 and 10 return to high ground in the middle of the course before 11 and 12 reverse back. The 13th is the second par 5, where you drive with a big carry from an elevated tee to a fairly generous fairway. The second shot, however, sees the fairway narrow dramatically as it runs steeply uphill to a small hidden green. It is both charming and testing.

The central area of the course, where the 10th tee and 11th and 14th greens meet, boasts a rather charming Swiss-chalet-style halfway hut. The 15th is a short Par 4 of just 300 yards but has a deep heathery chasm at 150 yards, (the hole is rather euphemistically called 'gully') therefore putting quite a lot of pressure on the tee shot and choices as to how to play the hole. 16 is the final Par 3 which plays alongside the Par 3 3rd in the opposite direction across the course. From the 17th tee there is a magnificent view over the Spey in the valley below, framed by the Cairngorms in the background. It is a tee where you would not mind being held up by players in front. 17 and 18 then head back downhill in similar style to the clubhouse.

The clubhouse benefited from considerable modernisation a few years ago, is now a very smart facility and has the appearance of being an important local meeting point which also welcomes visitors. There really is nothing not to like about Boat of Garten; it is a true Scottish golfing experience.

The 'Wee Course' at Blairgowrie; 2nd Green

This view of the 2nd hole looks back up the fairway from the back of the green. You can see the challenge that the charming 'nodding' firs represent. The hole is a dog-leg so if your drive is not very accurate the trees will make your second shot to the green extremely tricky.

Edradour Distillery

Edradour has a village feel to it with a series of low level buildings
set within a small hamlet. It is not as archetypal as Clynelish
in representing what an old distillery would have looked like
as the buildings have all been painted white with red doors
and windows. It does, however, give an attractive look.

CHAPTER FIVE

Perthshire

'It is well known that most Scotch and Irish Distilleries, as well as the interest they awaken as important sources of commercial interest, are invested with no ordinary attractions, by their picturesque surroundings and the magnificent country in which they are planted'

Alfred Barnard (1837-1918)

Historian and author of 'The Whisky Distilleries of the United Kingdom'

WE NOW HEAD south to Perthshire, often known as the 'Gateway to the Highlands'. It is also a staggeringly beautiful area with all of Scotland's famous types of landscape (except coastlines) concentrated in one: agricultural areas famous for fruit growing, rich forests, lochs and glens, and then the foothills of the Cairngorm mountains. Wherever you go you are never far from breath-taking scenery.

It also has a good representation of golf courses and distilleries without the former being as prevalent as in Fife or the latter as in Speyside. There are about seven distilleries from Deanstone, in Doune in the South, to Blair Atholl in the North. For golf courses, the world famous Gleneagles is the best known destination with the old King's and Queen's courses both being James Braid classics, while the new course became famous as the venue for the 2014 Ryder Cup. I have, however, gone to the north of Perthshire and chosen Edradour, near Pitlochry, as it claims to be Scotland's smallest working distillery (I say 'claims' because I am not sure that will remain the case) and as such represents a growing trend for 'small is beautiful' in the industry. It would have been easy alongside this to choose Pitlochry as the golf course. It is just a couple of miles away situated in the hills above the attractive town. It is a perfectly good course designed by an Open winner, Willie Fernie, and meets all the criteria of being an integral part of its surrounding environment. It also boasts a very active restaurant in the clubhouse which serves the wider community and tourist trade, as opposed to just golfers. But instead I have gone for Blairgowrie Golf Club. Arguably this stretches the definition of being 'geographically proximate' as it is over half an hour's drive from Edradour but, as I make the rules, I have decided that this qualifies if for no other reason than the drive between the two, which I will describe later, is a very special one.

From Speyside the quickest way to Pitlochry is down the A9. It is a road with dramatic scenery and takes you past Dalwhinnie, Scotland's highest distillery. An even more scenic (but much longer) route is from Tomintoul in the south of Speyside to Cockbridge on the infamous A939, which many may recognise from BBC traffic reports as normally the first road in Scotland to close when snow arrives. From there you take the A93 through Braemar into Perthshire; this is a bit of a detour but a rewarding one.

Pitlochry is an attractive little town with plenty of hotels and good quality bed and breakfast accommodation. There is plenty to do and see with the Pitlochry Festival Theatre attracting visitors throughout the year. Nearby Blair Atholl is also worth visiting with the Blair Castle and Gardens, the base of Europe's only private army.

Edradour nestles in the hills just beyond the village of Moulins east of Pitlochry. I have talked about the importance I attach to golf courses being in beautiful locations and it strikes me that I should also use this criterion with distilleries. Iain Banks in his book *Raw Spirit* makes the point: 'Many distilleries are quite beautiful. A lot, probably the majority, are set in scenery which is somewhere between rather lovely and utterly magnificent. There is, obviously, no link between the nobility of the distillery's environs or its architectural attractiveness and the worth of the whisky made there.' I am not so sure about the last sentence. Just as I believe that a golf course can be enhanced by its location, I can't help wondering whether there is some intangible influence on the quality of the spirit produced by the beauty of its surroundings.

Clynelish has a magnificent view down to the coast, Glenmorangie, though less well situated near the A9, does nonetheless look over the Dornoch Firth and up to the hills from where it gets its water. Benromach, despite the old world charm of its buildings, is disappointingly situated on a small industrial estate, while in contrast Glenlivet's slightly characterless buildings are made up for by the majesty of its setting in the Cairngorms. Here at Edradour the setting seems appropriate; it is a pretty Perthshire glen, small-scale buildings in small-scale scenery. This link between the scenery and the distillery was also made by Alfred Barnard in his seminal 1887 work on the whisky industry, which is still one of the few comprehensive guides to distilleries across Scotland and Ireland. He finds that most distilleries 'are invested with no ordinary attractions, by their picturesque surroundings and the magnificent country in which they are planted' and makes the case for the location being part and parcel of the experience very much as I have done for golf courses. I will pay more attention to this in future.

Edradour's history dates back to 1825 when it was set up as a farmers' cooperative moving to buildings on the current site in the 1830s. It has had an interesting, and at times chequered, history. There were a number of owners throughout the 19th and early 20th centuries before it was bought by J. G. Turney and Sons and became a major supplier of its 'House of Lords' and 'King's Ransom' blended whisky brands. Then in 1938 an American, allegedly with mafia connections, became the major shareholder. Edradour whisky was the main whisky in the famous incident in 1941 when a boat sank off the island of Eriskay taking 20,000 cases down with it. The story of the sinking, and the locals who looted the wreckage, was told in the book by Compton Mackenzie which was subsequently made into the film *Whisky Galore.*

An American/Australian consortium bought the distillery in 1976 subsequently selling it on in 1982 to Pernod Ricard (the current owners of Glenlivet). The first single malt was not introduced until 1986 and then Pernod Ricard sold the distillery onto Andrew Symington, the current owner, in 2002. I suspect that Pernod Ricard struggled with the small scale yet it was this feature which so attracted the new owner. He immediately brought in an operations director from Laphroaig, one of the famous Islay distilleries, and focused on single malts. The distillery produces in one year what the likes of Glenlivet produces in a week, so has to make the most of its distinctive character.

The distillery is in a very pretty setting and well geared up for visitors. The buildings have been carefully restored and new warehousing sympathetically added. Andrew Symington has even invested in on-site bottling, as he also owns a business called 'Signature Brands' which produces one-off specials malts from many of Scotland's famous distilleries.

The small scale makes the telling of how whisky is made fairly easy to follow. What they are most proud of is the way they cool the wort after the Mash Tun using a 'Morton refrigerator', which is now unique within the industry as the last one being used. In fact it is very new as they had to replace the old one and had this new one purpose built. It adds to the story even if it doesn't really change the product. The stills, however, being very small (the second one is again claimed to be Scotland's smallest) will have an impact on the product as the percentage of product directly exposed to the copper is obviously larger. The distillery maintains other traditional features such as removing the 'draff' (the used barley grains out of the mash tun) by tractor.

It strikes me that another similarity between golf and whisky is that they both have their own 'language'. Both have words and expressions which are unique to that activity. I'm conscious in this book of not assuming knowledge of 'mash tuns', 'wash backs', 'wort', 'draff' and expressions such as 'the angels' share'. Golf is the same; while some of the older names for clubs (mashies, brassies, niblicks and spoons) have largely been lost, there are still many technical terms; foursomes, four-balls, greensomes, medal play, matchplay and stableford as well as pars, birdies, eagles and albatrosses, which in America are called double eagles (which makes no sense mathematically – if an eagle is two under par, surely a double eagle should be four under par?). Incidentally, it was only recently that I learned that there is a word for four under par; a condor. This would require getting a hole in one at a Par 5 hole so I'm not sure it has ever been achieved – I suppose a condor is just a bigger and rarer form of an albatross. Anyway, I find considerable charm in these distinctive lexicons; they are not intended just for experts but enable shared values and experience between enthusiasts. They are very comforting.

At Edradour, it all adds up to a good story even, if much of it is done for effect. Andrew Symington understands the importance of marketing. The tour is well organised for tourists; you are greeted by a kilted guide (though I noticed some of the staff sported not only a kilt but a mixture of accents from eastern European to Australian!). The stated aim of the artisanal approach, using traditional processes, is to produce the same product as was produced 150 years ago, but to be honest, who knows? The bottle tells you that 'the men of Edradour follow the standards of those who have gone before. Only three in number, as there always have been, they continue to produce the finest single malt whisky available'. Compare this with Glenmorangie, which according to its bottle 'has been made in a steady, unhurried way, in an unchanging environment, by a small team of devoted craftsmen – the sixteen Men of Tain for over 150 years'. It is interesting that Glenmorangie had the sixteen Men of Tain to make the product while Edradour manages with just three!

Edradour claims to have 'a delicious aroma of sugared almonds and a hint of oloroso. The smooth, creamy, light malty taste is followed by a mellow, warming finish'. I first tasted it the evening before I visited the distillery when I was staying at a bed and breakfast in Pitlochry. I was relaxed, had eaten well and enjoyed it immensely, and though I hadn't read this description I could certainly have related to it. The following morning I was by myself and driving so only able to take the smallest of sips, which wasn't quite the same. As I say, it is all about context. The marketing story is a nice one and is part of the product, but again I wonder whether in a blind tasting I could name these different whiskies? Andrew Symington has also decided to produce a peated malt under a separate brand, Ballechin. This product is different, but then again, how different from an Islay peated malt? Is a peated malt from Perthshire really different from a peated malt from Islay? I am certainly learning that whisky is both a subtle and complex product.

This reminds me of golf balls. There is a similar mystique around the marketing of golf balls. There are many different brands and each brand, understandably, wants to tell you that its ball is better. Now for a golf ball there are essentially two features which players want; first, for the ball to go further and, secondly, for it to display good control around the greens. There can be a trade-off between these two things; harder balls go further while softer balls take more spin and therefore give more control. Most golf balls claim to do both! One brand markets four different balls which presumably have slightly different characteristics – some are softer than others. But the descriptions on these four balls on their distance capabilities are as follows; 'exceptional distance', 'outstanding distance', 'explosive distance' and 'impressive distance'. These balls have respectively 'more short game spin and control', 'excellent stopping control', 'playable feel' and 'good short game playability'. Aside from the rather clumsy, technical golfing language, it is essentially the same with whisky; most will want to claim to be 'smooth', 'mellow' and 'delicate'. Maybe it is because I am a marketing man by trade but I do find it amusing and therefore, while I enjoy the carefully written stories about each brand, I remain a little sceptical.

To get to Blairgowrie, do not return to Pitlochry from Edradour but instead turn right out of the lane at the end of the distillery and take the A924 via Bridge of Cally. You immediately climb steeply into the Cairngorms and are confronted with dramatic barren scenery and spectacular views. The road reaches some 1,200 feet within a few miles with sheep roaming everywhere. It is a delightful drive. As you descend down towards Bridge of Cally you return to lusher, more agricultural vistas as you meet the A94 which will take you to Blairgowrie.

Blairgowrie is not as pretty a town as Pitlochry being more agricultural in feel. The Golf Club is on the southern side sited in dense woodland of pine and silver birch and is certainly attractive. So why have I chosen Blairgowrie? It is one of Scotland's best inland courses and has a famous history. It is also a proper Scottish club and, despite its high profile and great heritage, caters for all the community. Finally, I wanted to include a course designed by Alister Mackenzie, the course designer who was responsible for some of the world's most famous courses from Augusta, to Cypress Point in California (generally regarded as much superior to its more famous neighbour, Pebble Beach) and Royal Melbourne in Australia. Mackenzie was an interesting character who liked to dress in a kilt and was proud of being Scottish, though he was actually born in Yorkshire to Scottish parents and educated at Wakefield Grammar School before reading medicine at Cambridge. He became a practicing doctor in Leeds and fought in the Boer

War before becoming one of the greats of golf course design. He died in California in 1934 in the same year that his famous Masters course at Augusta National started hosting the tournament that has now become such an important event in the golf calendar. Indeed he never saw Augusta fully completed.

Reading Mackenzie's views on course design, it is apparent he comes from the 'naturalist' tradition and is, in my view, similar to one of my other favourites, Harry Colt (see next chapter). Mackenzie's designs are very visual. Take some of his writings: 'the chief object of every golf architect is to imitate the beauties of nature'; 'while always keeping uppermost the provision of a splendid test of golf, I have striven to achieve beauty'. He was also an advocate of golf being essentially an enjoyable pastime (hence the importance of beauty) and so courses should not be punishing. 'It is an important thing in golf to make holes look much more difficult than they really are. People get more pleasure in doing a hole which looks almost impossible and yet is not so difficult as it appears.' Mackenzie hated punitive rough as it slowed the game down and people don't like looking for balls. Hazards such as bunkers are not there to punish but to make the golf 'more interesting'. It is a subtle but relevant distinction.

Today the Blairgowrie Club has three courses (two 18s – Rosemount and the Lansdowne, and a 9 hole called, rather appealingly, 'the Wee Course') and the history is complicated. The original main course dating from 1889 comprised just 9 holes and was called the Lansdowne with Mackenzie implementing his designs in the 1920s to make the new 18. In 1930, the club called in James Braid (yes, him again) to devise a new layout and make provision for a new 9 holes. Braid used some of the Mackenzie holes plus some new ones and the remaining 9 hole course became what today is the Wee Course. The new course was re-named 'Rosemount'. In the 1970s a second new 18 hole course was designed by Peter Alliss and Dave Thomas and was confusingly called The Lansdowne! This course used two holes from Rosemount so two new holes were also added to it. As I said, it is quite complicated.

So what is the result? Well, I haven't played the Lansdowne but it has to be said that its design was not without controversy at the time and even today many members don't like it. Most people say that the best two holes are the two pinched from Rosemount! It is, I gather, longer and narrower and tougher. From what I have heard it is a very good course but I am not in a hurry to play it. Rosemount itself is lovely, though its highlights come early and late. The first two holes and the last four are particularly memorable. In between there are some good holes, but some are quite similar, while the two new ones, built at the time of the new Lansdowne, are noticeably 'not quite the same'. The first hole, a relatively long Par 4, has an appealing shape to it with a gathering fairway leading to a tricky green. The second is much shorter but the approach to the green needs to be accurate. The last four all have appeal; 'Wee Dint' is a very short Par 3 to a well-protected green beside a beautiful loch which suddenly appears within the forest. On the next hole, depending on the tee, you drive either along the side of this loch (Black Loch) or over the corner to a strong right to left uphill dog-leg with a difficult long second to the green. The 17th is a longer Par 3 played across a gully to another well-protected green amongst the heather and trees, and the final hole is a dog-leg Par 4 back to the clubhouse with an annoyingly positioned oak tree on the dog-leg. All are good holes and very pretty ones.

As I said I haven't played The Lansdowne as the members seem less proud of it. By contrast, they all said that the Wee Course is a real hidden gem. The owner of the bed and breakfast where I stayed in Pitlochry said it was the best 9 hole course in Scotland so I made sure I did play it. And I was not disappointed. It is a real delight. It is undoubtedly 'wee'; 5 Par 4s and 4 par 3s. The Par 4s are not (with the exception of the 8th) long. But it is very 'classic'. The turf is magnificent – if anything better than on Rosemount. Two holes in particular stand out; the second, which is a lovely dog-leg Par 4 played down towards a green guarded by two large 'nodding' fir trees, which almost form an arch across the front of the green. The Par 3 7th is then not unlike Wee Dint on Rosemount, but this time played down into a small dell. It is a lovely way to spend an hour and a quarter, as that is all it will take you to play it.

The club has many claims to fame; in 1977 it held the European Tour Martini Tournament which was won by Greg Norman (his first tour victory); Gary Player was the Guest of Honour at the club's centenary celebrations in 1989; in 2014 the junior Ryder Cup was held at the club the week before the main event at Gleneagles. The club's most illustrious member was Jesse Valentine MBE, three times winner of the British Ladies' Amateur Championship (as far apart as 1937 and 1958!) and a regular Curtis Cup player. In 2014, club member Bradley Neil won the Amateur Championship, the first victory by a Scot in ten years.

The clubhouse has recently been extended but has maintained its elegant look. Part of this extension has meant that the changing rooms have moved upstairs with the catering now all done downstairs. This means that the best views of the course are actually from the windows of the changing rooms which offer a marvellous aspect down the first hole and the 18th green. I can think of only one other view from changing rooms in Scotland and that is the new links at Castle Stuart where the Men's showers are cleverly designed to enable you to watch the putting on the 9th green as you do your ablutions. I am assured this does not work reciprocally for those putting!

The Blairgowrie Golf Club is a great example of a classic Scottish club but one which has developed with the times; it has a rich history but is no longer in any way elitist and has become an important part of the community. In this way it is a model for many golf clubs.

The Eden at St Andrew's; 1st hole

The opening hole on The Eden is a typical Harry Colt opening
hole; a gentle introduction, though visually it can be deceptive
and judging distance can be tricky. In contrast to, say, Brora
or Boat of Garten, the scenery here is also much more 'gentle',
perhaps lacking drama, but it is always pleasant and arresting.

Anstruther in Fife

Antstruther (which is meant to be pronounced 'Ain ster') is a delightful fishing village in what is called the East Neuk ('Neuk' is a Scot's word for corner) of Fife. The waterfront and harbour are very pretty and you can take birdwatching trips out to the Isle of May famous for its puffins.

CHAPTER SIX

The Kingdom
Of Fife

'God made golf holes; it is the duty of the architect to find them'

Donald Ross (1872-1948)

Dornoch born golf course designer famed for
creating many American courses

IT IS A pleasant drive from Blairgowrie to Fife. Head south past Scone Palace and Perth, onto the A94 and there are a number of options for turning left into Fife. The first one takes you along the south coast of the Tay Estuary through Newburgh where the Fife coastal walk starts. This is becoming an increasingly popular attraction. From there you can head inland to Cupar and then quickly into St Andrews.

So why is Fife a 'Kingdom'? This dates back to the first millennium when Fife was the seat of the Pictish kings. From the 11th century, Dunfermline became the centre of the Scottish monarchy retaining this position for some 400 years. St Andrews became established in the 12th century with its cathedral, while the university, the oldest in Scotland, was founded in the early 15th century. Today Fife is a large region, stretching from Dunfermline in the west through the less attractive centre around Kirkcaldy and the new town of Glenrothes, to the rural farming lands around Cupar and the beautiful southern and eastern coastal areas. Apart from St Andrews there are some delightful towns and villages along the coast; Elie, Anstruther and Crail being the best examples and all worth visiting.

For golf we are spoilt. Not only is there St Andrews, 'the home of golf', where today there are some ten courses, but there are also great courses all along the coast from Kingsbarns to Crail, Elie, Lundin Links and Leven Links. There are also two noteworthy inland courses, Scotscraig and Ladybank, the latter of which is in many ways a match for the Rosemount at Blairgowrie and being situated only a few miles from my chosen distillery made a strong case for inclusion. In all there are, I think, 48 courses in the Kingdom. In the end I felt that I had to choose a course in St Andrews itself given its unique status in the golfing world. It should also be one of The Links Trust's courses (the main courses in St Andrews are not owned by any club but run by The Links Trust on behalf of the town.) The famous Old Course would not qualify given my criteria of being easy and relatively cheap for a visitor to play (though it has to be said that it is not that difficult to get a game on it if you have a handicap below 20). I rejected the new Castle Course, so was left with the three main other ones; the 'New', the Jubilee and the Eden. I think they are all a delight to play. The New (I just love a course which was opened in 1895 being called 'the New') is situated next door to the Old but is less quirky. Some say it lacks a bit of personality but it is always good. The Jubilee, which sits between the New and the sea, has been much improved over the years, most recently by Donald Steel, and is now a match for its neighbour. But I have chosen

The Eden for a number of reasons. It is the prettiest of all the St Andrews courses, being situated at the end of the estuary but still retaining a view of the famous town. It is probably the least booked-up because being slightly (only slightly) out of town, it is sometimes forgotten. But the other reason is that I was very keen to include a course designed by Harry Colt and that is not so easy in Scotland. The only other I know of is Muirfield which would not fit my criteria.

When I started researching the idea for this book I was confronted with the thought that there were no malt whisky distilleries in Fife. I then read that one called Daftmill was opening near Cupar, having been granted its distilling licence on St Andrew's Day in 2005. By the time I visited, a couple of years later, no fewer than five existed, either actually or in the planning stage; a new one was being built in Glenrothes in a joint venture between an Indian drinks group and a Perthshire distiller; an application has been made at Lindores Abbey, in the north near Newburgh to build a distillery on neighbouring farmland; a new distillery was opened at Kingsbarns next to the golf course, with an impressive visitor centre; and a micro-brewery called Eden Mill based in an old paper mill in Guardbridge, which had diversified out of beer to distilling gin had also decided to distil a small amount of whisky. So in no time I had a choice of five. By the time you read this there will probably be more. There is no coincidence in this trend I feel. This is Scotland marketing itself in an area which, because of its golf attracts a huge number of overseas visitors. The Glenrothes distillery shows the importance of the Asian market; the Kingsbarns distillery is unashamedly aimed at the golfers visiting the famous Kingsbarns course next door (it perhaps is more 'visitor centre' than 'distillery'), while Eden Mill is a micro-drinks marketing exercise again strongly geared to tourism. I know that at least two of these enterprises received big grants from the Scottish Government. But I am going to feature Daftmill because I think it is the most authentic of the five as you will see.

Daftmill is situated in a farming area called the 'Bow of Fife' just west of Cupar. It is only a few miles from Falkland Palace, the country home of the Stuart monarchs for over 200 years, which boasts the country's oldest real tennis court, built for King James V. The Cuthbert family claim to have been farming, and specifically growing barley, in this region of Fife for six generations. Having previously been tenants of the land, they bought the Pitlair Estate in 1984 from the Walker family who had owned it since the early 18th century. The current owner, Francis Cuthbert, when asked what prompted him to set up this enterprise shrugs his shoulders and seems almost embarrassed, suggesting the decision was made in a weak moment. But there is so much to admire in what he has achieved. His distillery is housed in attractive old farm buildings and he also matures the spirit on site. He has invested a huge amount of money (without government grants – distilleries, unlike visitor centres, don't employ many people) in high quality equipment, he has a passion for producing a quality product and will not compromise on this, he has a genuine local provenance story and strong environmental credentials. I think it is a shame that such enterprises do not receive government support – it may not directly employ many people but think of the suppliers of the equipment. The problem is new micro-distilleries are a lousy business model.

You have to invest and wait 10 years to sell your product. It's a cash flow disaster. That is why there are so many micro-breweries and now micro-gin distilleries. They can invest and sell immediately. Not so with quality malt whisky.

Gin's association with Scotland is less well recognised as it is generally regarded as being quintessentially 'English'. There is 'London gin' and 'Plymouth gin' but actually over 70 per cent of the gin consumed in the UK is manufactured in Scotland. Three of the world's best known brands (Hendrick's, Tanqueray and Gordon's) are made in Scotland, the latter two being owned by Diageo, emphasising the link between the two drinks. The making of good gin spirit essentially requires the same skills as making good whisky spirit. The difference is that gin doesn't mature so can be sold immediately, hence its cash flow advantages. Also it does not have the same legislative constraints as whisky. There are no restrictions on added ingredients to impart a particular flavour. It is therefore a much less complex product and less mysterious. The market, however, is booming, with gin sales predicted to overtake those of Scotch whisky in the next few years. This has encouraged lots of small distillers to compete with the internationally marketed brands so the market has diversified in the same way as malt whisky, and small Scottish businesses like Eden Mill in St Andrews (and North Berwick Gin and Edinburgh Gin and Orkney Gin) are leading the way – it is estimated that over 30 gin companies are now operating in Scotland.

I hope that Francis is hugely successful. I think the distinctive name is an asset. The story is that the local burn, because of the topography of the land, had the appearance of flowing uphill and so became known as the 'daft' burn and the mill then being called 'Daft Mill'. Francis seemed slightly to eschew 'marketing' his products though he would be unwise not to make the most of the distinctive name and the genuine local story of using barley and water from the farm. He is committed to a small scale so will need to sell at a premium and his approach to product quality supports this. Put it this way, this product will not be on offer in Tesco. I obviously can't tell you what it is like because at the time of writing it had not been released. Maybe he should have looked at also producing a gin to help the business, but his interest is in whisky and I have no doubt that he doesn't want to dilute that focus. He says that he hopes the product will sell itself and it is clear that he sees his market as the connoisseur whisky enthusiast looking for a high quality and distinctive product. He mentions Scandanavia as an interesting market in this respect. This reminds me of a bar I visited in the small university town of Lund in Sweden which had the largest malt whisky menu I have ever seen. Very often the real connoisseurs of Scottish malt whisky are not Scottish.

It is a relatively short drive of about half an hour to St Andrews along the A91 through the attractive small market town of Cupar. As you come into St Andrews the Eden is in fact the first course that you see and a left turn takes you into the impressive new clubhouse which serves the Eden, Strathtyrum and Balgove courses. The Links Trust was established by Act of Parliament back in 1974 and has become an extremely professional organisation over the past 20 years. All the seven courses are public but 25 years ago a visit to St Andrews as a private golfer was a slightly haphazard experience. The first clubhouse was not built until 1995 serving the New and Jubilee courses as well as being a facility for visitors playing the Old.

The clubhouse for the Eden was then completed in 1997. As a visitor to any of the courses you are now properly looked after. The clubhouse facilities are excellent, the staff who greet you enthusiastic, knowledgeable and professional. It is a slick operation. Before talking about the Eden it is worth just saying a few words about playing 'the Old'. You can book in advance but this has to be done in late August/early September for the following calendar year and you are not guaranteed specific dates and times. The other way is to enter the daily ballot and if you are in the area for a few days this is well worth doing because depending on the time of year your chances are quite high. You need to put your name down two days before you want to play and find out that evening if you have been successful. You simply need to be a club member with a handicap of 20 or better. It is in this respect a very democratic process.

The Old is an extraordinary course. It breaks most rules of a great design. There are only two par 3s and two Par 5s. A fascinating piece of trivia is that it is the only course in the world with a 'palindromic par pattern' – 4,4,4,4,5,4,4,3,4,4,3,4,4,5,4,4, 4,4! (If anyone can find another one please let me know). There are lots of quite short and, on the face of it, quite uninteresting Par 4s. At times it looks quite bland. I have heard many golfers express slight disappointment after playing it for the first time as they had expected something more dramatic. But it is in fact a remarkable test of golf, though for the top players, like most links courses, it needs a wind to be a really tough test. Alister Mackenzie wrote:

'A good golf course is like good music; it is not necessarily a course that appeals the first time one plays over it, but one which grows on the player the more frequently he visits it.'

This is certainly true of the Old Course and the analogy is a good one. I found that with composers like Mahler and Bruckner – you need familiarity to appreciate them fully. And I think it is true with some malt whiskies also; at first a new malt may taste just like any other malt. But try it a few times and you get to know it. I am certainly finding that. As with golf, I need more practice.

It is much easier to play the Eden and indeed if you visit St Andrews enter the ballot and are disappointed, there will still be a chance of getting on the Eden at a couple of days' notice. You won't be disappointed. While the Eden is the only course I have selected which isn't really a 'club' (though The Machrie on Islay, while having a club, is not owned by it) the experience of playing it almost makes it feel like one. The smart clubhouse has a shop and good dining facilities. The scorecard is also smart with the Eden given its own logo – the lovely and distinctive small stone cottage at the back of the first green. I always like clubs which make an effort with their scorecards and club logos. It was good to see Brora, in celebrating its 125th Anniversary, updating its club logo – the artic tern. The use of birds or animals on club logos is popular. Machrihanish, which we visit in Chapter 8, uses the oystercatcher. Others will use club crests along with depictions of golf clubs which can be rather generic and disappointing. I like those that are distinctive and relevant to a local feature; Tain uses St Duthac who founded the town and whose birthplace was allegedly where the golf course now is. Moray features the lighthouse which is such an important feature of its landscape. The most disappointing on this tour was Boat of Garten which has a rather contrived logo encompassing a B and a G and a golf club and ball. It looks as if it has been created by a GCSE art student. But quality of logo does not necessarily correlate with quality of club. Many of the top ones have rather predictable crests – Royal Portrush, Royal Lytham, Royal Troon for example. But I prefer those which use either a local landmark or relevant wildlife; the white goats at Lahinch, a hare at Waterville, signature trees at Sunningdale and Carnoustie, birds at Portmarnock and Royal Liverpool. I recently played at Newquay which uses a Cornish chough, though the local I played with had to admit that the likelihood of seeing one on the course nowadays is extremely remote!

Daftmill Distillery

So who was Harry Colt and why am I a fan of his designs? Colt attended Cambridge University at the same time as Mackenzie, though there is no evidence that they met there. Colt was heavily involved in golf at Cambridge and was the first captain of the Cambridge University club. He left to become a lawyer and set up a practice in Hastings. From there he started on his first famous design at Rye. In 1902 Colt applied for a job at the R&A and surprisingly was turned down despite many recommendations, including allegedly one from no less than A. J. Balfour, the future Prime Minister. However, it was not long before Colt became Secretary at a prestigious new course, Sunningdale, being appointed in 1902 to the post from a field of some 400 applicants. The course had recently been completed and was designed by Willie Park Junior. Colt made a few final amendments and also went on to design the New Course there. Over the next decade, Colt began to take an increasing interest in course design. In 1910 he asked to leave Sunningdale but was persuaded to stay on with an assistant appointed. Eventually he left and devoted the rest of his career to course design, working not only with Mackenzie but others such as Herbert Alison and John Morrison, both of whom became well -known names in the growing business of golf course architecture.

The Eden is one of his earlier designs, dating from before the Great War. I am a great fan of Colt courses (my own club, Beaconsfield, was also an early Colt design) and he designed many of the famous old parkland and heathland courses around London; Moor Park, Stoke Poges, St George's Hill, Royal Wimbledon, Swinley Forest and Wentworth as well as Sunningdale New.

Mackenzie described the Eden as the 'best artificially con- structed seaside course I know' making the point that Colt was working with the least interesting piece of links land available as the best parts had already been used for the Old, the New and the Jubilee. At the same time as designing the Eden, Colt was asked to make recommendations on both the Old and the New and wrote an extensive report, so even these courses are likely to have some of his influences. The Eden may not be in the top drawer of links courses, and it is true that the links land it occupies is not dramatic in any way, but it is always entertaining with some great holes and some very distinctive features. Like Mackenzie, Colt was an early 'naturalist' and this can be seen on the Eden. Colt felt that course designers should always remember that golf is, as he put it, 'a pastime and not a penance'. This was not a call for making courses easy. He felt that enjoyment required providing 'plenty of difficulty but surely there is no need for vindictiveness'. Colt was also an early advocate of designing courses which would suit several standards of golfers and he always had this in mind. It was Colt who first developed the now common feature of having several different teeing positions so that a hole can be played at a number of different lengths. Placement of hazards can also be designed to, for example, only affect the longer hitters.

Colt was a very subtle designer and used visual tricks. Very often by placing the green in a certain position he made it look nearer than it actually is. He was also famous for placing bunkers just short of the green, as opposed to adjacent, which creates the same effect. Visual hazards can be as tough as physical ones. Most of his fairway bunkers were positioned for risk/reward. The best position from which to play your second shot will be near the fairway bunker. Play safe to ensure that you avoid the bunker and your second shot will be more difficult. The choice is yours.

It has to be said that today's Eden is not all Colt's work as a number of revisions were made by Donald Steel to enable the two new courses to be accommodated nearby. There are two holes in particular (14 and 15) which are played alongside a pond on land which, though right next to the estuary, does not have a 'links feel'. But the majority of Colt's creation remains and there are a number of Colt features. It is very traditional in style and has been designed compactly without using an enormous amount of land. I like the fact that the walks from the greens to the next tees are invariably very short. With a lot of modern courses, designers look to find the next hole on a nearby piece of land but this can involve long treks between holes. I always find this annoying and it also adds significantly to the time taken to play a round. It should really be obvious from the green where the next hole is. The design format of the Eden is Colt's favourite two loops of 9, one clockwise and the other anti-clockwise, probably most famously present at Muirfield. This is a great feature for a links course where wind is a factor because it means the wind direction is always changing. On 'out and back' formats, there tends to be long stretches of holes either into or with the wind behind. The best holes are probably all on the front 9, being the two relatively short par 4s (4 and 7) and two quirky Par 3s (5 and 8) with neighbouring greens which make the most of what look like natural dune features but which may have had some Colt influence. The two Par 3s are also interesting in that the tee shots for each cross each other; i.e. the 5th green is on the right of the 8th green but is played from a tee which is alongside, but to the left of, the 8th tee! It can cause some confusion. The most famous hole is probably the 7th with a risk/reward drive to a slope on a slight dog-leg alongside the estuary. Left is the estuary, there are whins on the right and the slope can make a slightly misguided shot kick off the fairway. The green is then precariously placed and well-guarded, so even if your drive is good and you are left with a short pitch, the job is by no means done.

There are some tough long holes too with 2, 3 and 11 usually into the prevailing wind and requiring two very good shots to get home in two. The 3rd green and 4th tee is a lovely spot overlooking the estuary; you can see most of the course in front of you and you can look back beyond the Old Course and see the town in the background. It is a very rewarding experience.

So Fife contains the oldest of golf courses and the newest of distilleries and there are signs, with the likes of the Kingsbarns and Eden Mill distilleries, that the developing whisky industry will use the region's rich golfing heritage as a means of marketing its Scottish provenance. It makes good sense.

Kilspindie Golf Club; 8th hole

Alister Mackenzie said that a good designed hole should look more
difficult than it actually is. This Par 3 is a good example. There
is a bunker short and the beach to the right. The green is bigger
than it looks from the tee so a solid shot has plenty of room.
But then it is a links course and there is always the wind…

The Whisky Museum at Glenkinchie

This museum at Glenkinchie near Edinburgh is a central part of the distillery visit and as well as containing a number of interesting historical artefacts gives the novice a good introduction to how whisky is made. The other museum worth visiting is located in an old distillery, Dallas Dhu, near Forres in Moray.

CHAPTER SEVEN

East Lothian

'Hard by, in the fields called the Links, the citizens of Edinburgh divert themselves at a game called Golf, in which they use a curious kind of bats tipped with horn, and small elastic balls of leather, stuffed with feathers, rather less than tennis balls, but of much harder consistence. These they strike with such force and dexterity from one hole to another, that, they will fly to an incredible distance. Of this diversion the Scots are so fond that, when the weather will permit, you may see a multitude of all ranks, from the senator of justice to the lowest tradesman, mingled together, in their shirts, and following the balls with the utmost eagerness.'

Tobias Smollett (1721-1771)

The Links of Leith, from the novel,
The Expedition of Humphrey Clinker (1771)

 OUR NEXT DESTINATION, East Lothian, is less than 20 miles as the crow flies across the Firth of Forth (at its narrowest, between Elie and North Berwick, the Firth is less than 10 miles across) but the trip takes much longer than you might expect, as you have to head west across the Forth Road Bridge and then back east, past Edinburgh, a journey of nearly two hours. East Lothian, not unlike Fife, is another mini golfing paradise. There aren't quite as many courses as in Fife, but

in a short stretch of coastline from Musselburgh to Dunbar, a distance of some 30 miles, I can count no less than 20 golf courses. Indeed, we are headed to a short strip of this coastline from Aberlady through Gulllane to North Berwick, no more than eight miles long, where 11 of these courses are situated.

East Lothian also has much else to commend it; a surprisingly dry climate, lots of history, tremendous birdwatching, both in Aberlady Bay and on the many islands just off the coast, and some delightful scenery. North Berwick is probably the best known resort town on the coast, sitting below Berwick Law, a volcanic plug of rock which rises to some 600ft just behind the town. On top was a famous landmark, a whale's jawbone which was put there in the 18th century. In 2005 it collapsed having rotted away, and has now been replaced with a fibreglass replica. The town is also the home of the Scottish Seabird Centre and you can take trips out to the surrounding islands, all of which boast colonies of many rare seabirds. The Bass Rock, home to nesting gannets is the most distinctive and famous. It is white in colour as it is covered in gannets and their guano which gives it a remarkable look in the evening sun.

So the choice of golf course was very difficult. The most prestigious is undoubtedly the home of 'the Honourable Company of Edinburgh Golfers', Muirfield, but, magnificent though it is, as I have previously said, such a course and club does not fit my criteria. There are also a number of new links courses (Archerfield and The Renaissance for example) but you will have worked out by now that they are unlikely to be my choice. (I instinctively treat any golf club given the name 'The Renaisssance' with much suspicion). The oldest is the famous 9 hole links at Musselburgh which today sits in the middle of the racecourse. It was the home of Willie Park Senior, the winner of the first ever Open Championship, held at Prestwick in 1860.I was at school across the road and played there in the 1970s when it had fallen into disrepair with only some of the greens even boasting a flagstick. It has more recently been better looked after and recently I have read about plans to raise money to restore the course to its former glory and invest in the clubhouse facilities. In the end the choice came down to two: North Berwick, one of my favourite courses, and Kilspindie, a delightful old links overlooking Aberlady Bay.

North Berwick would have been the easy and less controversial choice. The original course designer is unknown but I know of few courses with so many memorable holes; from the quirky 1st with the green sitting precariously on top of a dune, to the 13th which has a brick wall across the front of the green (yes, a brick wall across the front of the green!). Then there is 'Perfection', the appropriately named 14th, where you play your second shot blind over a dune to a green sitting just above the beach, and the famous 'Redan' short 15th, which has been the inspiration for so many Par 3s around the world. Not to mention the bizarre green on the 16th which has a deep gully running across the middle, or the fairway on the 17th which has to be the 'bumpiest' in the world of golf. The 18th is reminiscent of the same hole on the 'Old' at St Andrews, a short Par 4 playing back towards the town and sharing a big wide fairway with the 1st but with, if anything, a more alarming out of bounds on the right, which is the Golf Club car park. There is charm and interest throughout. The setting, with the Bass Rock in the background and tremendous views of Fife across the Firth of Forth, is also beautiful. If you visit East Lothian you must play it.

If there is a negative to North Berwick it is that so many people understandably want to play it and it can be a bit slow, though the club do their best to ensure that their visitors keep to a sensible pace of play. Pace of play has become a big issue in golf and in my view is the reason behind a worrying decline in the sport's popularity, which is evident both in the UK and the US. I remember when I was playing as a teenager, a notice at North Berwick which simply stated that 'a round of gold should take no longer than two and three quarter hours'. I think it would be easier to market the sport to today's 'time poor' young if it simply was quicker to play. The Royal & Ancient Golf Club, the sport's governing body, is acutely aware of the issue and is looking at a number of measures to overcome it, including encouraging faster play and holding more 9 hole tournaments. You could argue that the trend to new three year old malt whiskies is addressing a similar problem!

A number of clubs are in financial trouble as supply now exceeds demand. Modern life is quite impatient; we all want to do everything instantly and quickly and a sport which takes at least half a day is at a big disadvantage. The problem with pace of play cannot be put down to too many people trying to play too few courses, but, the way people play. Amateurs tend to watch professionals and believe that they need to do everything that they do. That never used to be the case while there used to be a lot more foursome (two sets of two players playing the same ball alternatively), rather than fourball (two sets of two players playing their own ball), golf. But in this increasingly self-orientated world, playing your own ball has become the norm. I think golf, a bit like cricket, needs to

recognise the time factor and make shorter forms of the game more accessible. More 9 hole competitions and more foursome play are two potential solutions.

But back to East Lothian, I have chosen for this book, Kilspindie, a much less well-known course which may not be as memorable a pure golfing experience but for all round enjoyment from the course to its setting, the clubhouse and its history, for me typifies the best in Scottish golfing experience. For the distillery, there is only one; Glenkinchie. It is located in a pretty agricultural location, near the village of Pencaitland, just south-east of Edinburgh.

Glenkinchie is another Diageo distillery and represents their Lowland classic malt. Being so near to Edinburgh, it is one of the most visited distilleries, and it has a very extensive visitor centre, museum and shop. Its history dates back to 1827 when a licence was granted to two local farming brothers George and John Rate. It ceased production in the second half of the 19th century and was sold to a local farming family called Christie who converted the premises into a sawmill. Descendants of the Christie family remained working in the distillery over one hundred years later. Whisky production did not start again until the 1890s. For most of its history it has produced blends – it was the main source for the famous Haig Dimple brand – but its recent fame is down to United Distillers and Vinters (the business that was to become Diageo) choosing it as one of the six classic malts in 1988. Initially Glenkinchie was a 10-year-old, but since 2007 has been sold as a 12-year-old. It is a huge distillery and even today only about 10 per cent of the whisky produced goes to the Glenkinchie single malt.

The buildings are classic Victorian industrial architecture; imposing yet beautiful. Some parts are home to a colony of bats which are normally fairly fussy about the type of architecture they inhabit. There is the tell-tale sign that they are distillery buildings with the ever-present black mould which is created in the air from maturing spirit. They sit in a small valley amidst rolling farmland; a very peaceful setting. The floor maltings were closed in 1968, after which they were converted into the museum. While the business is owned by the mighty multinational Diageo, it continues to use other local resources. The barley is harvested locally and malted at Bairds in Pencaitland just down the road, while the fuel used remains coal which had been a flourishing industry in this part of East Lothian in the first half of the 20th century.

The visit is well organised and informative. The equipment is well invested as you would expect from a multinational owner but much of the traditional feel has been maintained with six wooden washbacks remaining, four made from Canadian larch and two from Oregon pine. The distillery has one of the largest stills in Scotland with a capacity of 32,000 litres – it is an impressive sight – something which allegedly is an important factor in Glenkinchie's mild and smooth taste. It is interesting to see in the warehouse a full range of barrels of Diageo whiskies; it is their policy to spread the stocks of their precious brands all around each of their distilleries. While it is clearly expensive to transport it is in fact a very cost-effective insurance policy. The museum is also worth the visit, especially for a whisky novice, as it not only explains the process but also the history of the industry.

It strikes me that there are many parallels in the histories of whisky and golf. If you go back to the 1890s, this was a boom

time for both industries. Since The Open had been established 30 years earlier, and the ensuing rivalries between the Morrises and the Parks had created much interest in the game, there became a huge demand for courses to be built and many famous ones date from this decade. In whisky too, the 1890s was a decade of considerable investment and corporate activity, with whisky becoming a strong export market. This has sometimes been put down to the phylloxera pest devastating the brandy industry in France during the 1880s allowing whisky to plug the resultant gap in the market. Here America was central to both industries with Scottish designers, for example Donald Ross, Willie Park Junior and Archie Simpson, all finding fame there. The 1890s was the decade which saw the Jack Daniels brand get fully established with the distinctive square shaped bottle first introduced in 1897.

The Bass Rock

Both whisky and golf suffered during the world wars of the first half of the 20th century while prohibition in America was clearly a further blow to whisky. Golf between the wars, by contrast, thrived, with the rate of course building continuing where it left off before the Great War. The 1920s were also the era of Bobby Jones and Walter Hagan, arguably the first golfing superstars. It was in the 1920s that the Ryder Cup started. It was America that dominated the game for the next half century, with Jones and Hagan being followed by famous names such as Hogan and Snead and then Palmer and Nicklaus. In fact it was these last two that led to the revival of the sport in the UK as they, and a number of other leading Americans, began to study and appreciate the history of the game and its links to Scotland in particular. Ben Hogan was the greatest player in the world for over two decades but only played in one Open Championship (which he won at Carnoustie in 1952). He largely played in America. It was the willingness of Palmer, from the late 1950s, to travel to play in the Open that revived the tournament so that it attracted a field containing the world's best players. This internationalisation of the game then took off in the 1970s. While Australia and South Africa (and to a lesser extent South America) had always had great players, there had been few from Europe or Asia. The last thirty years has seen this change dramatically with the 'European Tour' playing tournaments in Africa, the Middle East and Asia.

The fortunes of the whisky industry more recently have almost been countercyclical with those of golf; just as golf did well in the 1920s while whisky was suffering, in the period from 1950 to 1980 over 20 new distilleries were opened in Scotland with only a few closures. Then from 1980 to 2000, as golf grew and became truly global, the whisky market experienced over-capacity with over twenty distilleries closing and only two (Kininvie/Glenfiddich and Arran) opening. Since 2000 this trend has again reversed with over 20 opening and a considerable number of further ones proposed. While internationally golf has prospered, it has lost regular players and there is, in both America and the UK, overcapacity in courses leading to declining club memberships and some in America even closing.

When I first started drinking malt whisky fairly regularly about ten years ago, Glenkinchie became my brand of choice. I liked its pale look while its taste is drier, lighter and slightly sweeter than many other malts. I knew very little about malts at the time but I felt it suited me. It is perhaps less complex than others but then again, as I continue to say, much depends on your mood. The dryness is alleged to come from chalky deposits in the water used, which runs over limestone deposits in the neighbouring Lammermuir Hills. As I have said, I like these stories but still can't convince myself that they are true.

Kilspindie has an interesting history. The original golf club founded in 1867 was called 'Luffness Golf Club' and was situated on the east side of Aberlady Bay on land which is now part of the nature reserve. In the mid-1890s there was a proposal to move to a newly designed course nearer the neighbouring small town of Gullane. This caused a split in the club as it was unpopular with the Aberlady members. Thus two clubs were formed out of one; Luffness New was created just to the west of Gullane Hill (the club is still there today and is an excellent course with a very fine clubhouse) while the 'Old' Luffness moved to some new links land bordering Craigielaw Farm, donated by the Earl of Weymss. The course opened in 1898 and the club was renamed 'Kilspindie' in 1899. The nucleus of the current clubhouse dates from the 1898 opening and is one of the most characterful we will encounter on this trip. Architecturally it is nothing special but inside there are some lovely features. The main bar is the original locker room fully wood panelled with the narrow lockers (all bags were 'pencil bags' in 1898) and a bar hatch. Above the fireplace the central feature is the Honours Boards which includes some fine sounding names including the Prime Minister, A. J. Balfour. The rest of the clubhouse has been extended to give plenty of space and, while more modern in feel, is bright and welcoming. The clubhouse surrounds are very distinctive with little garden areas featuring a putting green, but also borders of flowers and various patios with seats. It is all very congenial.

Kilspindie will never be ranked in the top bracket as it is by modern standards very short at only 5,500 yards off the main tees. I am a great fan of short Par 4s but there are probably too many (six in total) for an ideal balance. And there is just the one Par 5; ideally you would want at least one more, but other than that this is classic links golf of the very best kind. The turf is tremendous, the greens well protected, the fairways have gentle undulations, the holes turn all directions and the wind is always a factor. And finally it is situated in a most beautiful spot on a small headland pointing out into the Firth of Forth. While it is only some seven miles from North Berwick the views are very different. The Bass Rock is hidden by Gullane Hill (though you can still see Berwick Law). Instead you have a delightful view of the nature reserve in Aberlady Bay just below Gullane Hill to the east and up to Edinburgh where the castle, Arthur's Seat and the rail and road bridges can be clearly seen. Arthur's Seat is actually the name of the third hole and is a good marker guide for what is a blind drive.

The course was designed by Willie Park Junior (yes, son of Willie Park Senior). The Park and Morris families dominated The Open in its early years, between them winning thirteen of the first fifteen championships. Willie Senior won three of the first seven, with brother Mungo (not the famous explorer from a century earlier – I assume they come from the same family but have not been able to verify this) then winning in 1874, before Willie Senior won his fourth and last the following year. Willie Junior then won two Opens in the late 1880s. The Parks of Musselburgh were great rivals of both Old Tom and Young Tom Morris; they used to hold big challenge matches and it was during one of these matches between the Parks and the Morrises at North Berwick in September 1875 that Young Tom received a telegram to say that his wife was seriously ill. He immediately took a yacht from North Berwick over the Forth estuary back to St Andrews to find that she had died in childbirth. Young Tom was devastated by the loss, became ill, as well as succumbing to heavy drinking, and himself died at the age of only 24 in December that year.

After winning his two Opens, Willie Junior, rather like Old Tom, became a course designer, initially in the UK and latterly in the US. He has a number of famous courses to his name, notably Sunningdale Old and Huntercombe in the south of England, Maidstone on Long Island, Weston in Toronto and Olympia Fields in Illinois. He also wrote one of the first instruction books on the game; *The Art of Golf.*

It is worth considering the impact that changing technology has had on the game and in particular the design of courses. The greater distances that the ball can now be hit has had an enormous effect on courses, many of which have been lengthened to accommodate this. At some courses, and on some holes, this is possible by simply moving the tee back. At Kilspindie, however, and on many other older courses, this would be impossible on the vast majority of holes as there simply is not the room. But it is difficult to design a course for the mid to low handicapper who hits a drive 250 yards as well as a professional who hits it perhaps 300 yards. And longer courses are not necessarily better ones; for the average golfer they just make a round of golf longer without necessarily being more enjoyable. I think the technological changes in clubs and balls which have enabled all players to hit the ball further have been a mixed blessing for the game. Interestingly this is not just a modern phenomenon as golf, like all sports, has always been impacted by technology changes going back to the introduction of the gutta percha ball which caused the split between Old Tom and his mentor Allan Robertson is the 1840s. The famous BBC golf commentator, Henry Longhurst, wrote about the issue in an article as long ago as the 1950s. He bemoaned the fact that new technology was always trying to make the balls go further and thereby compromising the original design of courses and making rounds take longer. 'What a farce is this business of length!….year by year we walk further and further…no one, as far as I can see, benefits and many lose'. What technology has done is to make the game easier for the higher handicap golfer as the clubs, as well as enabling the ball to be hit further, are more forgiving. You could argue that in this respect it has made the game less skilful.

The course starts unusually with a Par 3 playing away from the clubhouse directly out to the sea. It is a relatively benign looking hole but deceptively long – the great designers generally rely on slight optical illusions as a course defence. The next three holes (the only Par 5 followed by two tricky Par 4s) hug the coastline and offer all sorts of test, depending on the wind direction. The third tee shot is blind and has a difficult green, while the tee shot on the 4th needs to be accurate as does the approach, as the green is perched on a small promontory just above the beach. Look out for seals basking on the rocks all along this stretch. It is delightful – golf and the environment sitting naturally together, just as it should be. The holes turn back inland and then head out again along the bay to reach the famous 8th hole which is a fantastic Par 3. I don't really like the concept of a 'signature hole' but this would be Kilspindie's. You play across the corner of the beach over some sleepers to a green which looks small from the tee, though is actually reasonably generous when you reach it. Members talk about a two day assistant professionals' competition played at Kilspindie a few years back where there were holes-in-one at the 8th on both days; the first day it was with a 3 wood; the second day with a wedge. Such is Scottish links golf.

The holes then head back inland. There is one point on the course that typifies Kilspindie. Most of the tees, as is the tradition on old links courses, are very close to the previous green. As Kilspindie is a short course on an incredibly small piece of land for 18 holes, every square yard is used. There is an area in the middle of the course, on its highest point, where there are four tees and four greens all within about 50 yards of each other: the 3rd, 5th, 12th and 14th greens with (self-evidently!) the 4th, 6th, 13th and 5th tees. Everywhere you look there is golf being played; golfing hub-bub all around. It is just marvellous.

Kilspindie may not be a 'great' course but it is a great experience. It is a genuine local club where, as Tobias Smollett observed over two hundred years ago, 'the senator of justice' might play with 'the lowest tradesman'. It was clearly good enough for an ex-Prime Minister. The location is also wonderful; the views across the Forth and up to Edinburgh are endlessly diverting. There is certainly something special about a sea view with land in the distance as opposed to a coast where you simply look out to sea. It is this combination of the short aspect coastal views combined with the long aspect of the Fife coast in the distance that makes East Lothian so special.

Machrihanish Golf Club; 1st tee 'The Drive Across the Atlantic'
The view from the first tee at Machrihanish changes constantly
with the tides and the weather. When the tide is out you are
confronted by an expanse of beach. When it is in, the waves lap up
against the shore and the oystercatchers bob up and down on the
water. The hills in the distance present the perfect backdrop.

Dunaverty on the Southernmost Tip of the Mull of Kintyre

This is one of the quietest and prettiest spots on the Mull and
often missed by visitors. The small golf course sited around
Dunaverty Rock was where one of Scotland's most successful
amateur lady golfers, Belle Robertson, first learned to play.

CHAPTER EIGHT

Kintyre

'If an angel out of heaven
gives you something else to drink
thank her for her kind intention
and pour it down the sink'

G K Chesterton (1874-1936)

English writer, poet, philosopher and whisky lover

FOR THE FINAL two chapters we are headed over to the west coast. We are arguably passing by three areas which you would not want to miss on any tour of Scotland; the Borders, Dumfries and Galloway and the Ayrshire coast. There are however, problems with all of these. I was tempted to include the Borders as it is a beautiful part of the country and I grew up in Melrose in the heart of Border country. But in truth it has little in the way of famous golf courses or distilleries. However, again, as in Fife, there are signs of life. I know of three new projects to bring whisky distilling back to the Borders with one in Hawick, one in Jedburgh and another in Peebles. While the Borders boasts many small local golf clubs, many in beautiful surroundings, perhaps the best course is The Roxburghe, built about 20 years ago on the Duke of Roxburgh's estate. It is relatively unknown but a well laid out course in a delightful piece of countryside along the banks of the Tweed.

In Dumfries and Galloway, two distilleries which had been closed are now back in business; Bladnoch in Wigton went into administration in 2014 but has since been bought by an Australian businessman, while Annandale, an old producer of whisky for the Johnnie Walker brand, is now producing single malts. This latter distillery could be combined with the best course on the southern coast at Southerness, a links course opened after the Second World War, which affords beautiful views over the Solway Firth to the Lake District.

The Ayrshire coast is a haven of great golf courses from the historic Prestwick, home of the first six Open Championships, to the famous modern day Open venues of Turnberry and Troon, to the less famous but great Western Gailes and even the new modern links at Dundonald. The issue is distilleries. There used to be a very big Johnnie Walker bottling plant in Kilmarnock while there is still a big William Grant Grain distillery at Girvan and they have opened a small malt distillery called Ailsa Bay next door. Let's await developments in all these areas and instead head for an area which can offer greatness in both.

The Mull of Kintyre is in many ways defined by its geography. Campbeltown, where we are headed for our distillery, and Machrihanish, our next golfing destination, are no more than sixty miles from Glasgow as the crow flies. By road it will take you a good three hours as you have to head up Loch Lomond, cross to the top of Loch Long and drive due south. It is a long way but worth the journey. A stop in the delightful village of Inveraray with its famous castle, the seat of the Duke of Argyll, and its historic jail, makes a good break in the trip. Another option is to take the Caledonian McBrayne ferry from Ardrossan to Campbeltown which operates about three times a week in the summer. It is not much quicker than driving, also taking over three hours, but, weather permitting, it is a spectacular trip. I last did it on a June evening, leaving Ardrossan at six o'clock in the evening. The sea was like a millpond and you start with the sun over the considerable hills of Arran to the west. The route then takes you down past the southern tip of Arran and you see the famous Ailsa Craig rock to the east. This is the famous landmark you see off the coast at Turnberry; indeed the main course at Turnberry used to be called the 'Ailsa' (with the second course called 'the Arran'). It is a remarkable plug of rock, only 240 acres in size, and reputably the source of the best granite for making curling stones. The ferry journey then heads west past the south end of Arran and across to the south end of the Kintyre peninsular and Campbeltown harbour where, by the arrival time of 9.20pm, I was greeted by a dramatic sunset.

Arran itself is worth a quick mention as it could certainly qualify for a chapter. There are in fact seven golf courses on Arran which, with a population of just about 5,000, is quite impressive. Three are 18 holes, three are 9 holes, but the most famous is Shiskine which has 12 holes. The history is complicated as it was once a 9 hole course and then an 18 hole course before the club lost some land and was left with 12 holes. To describe the course as 'quirky' is something of an understatement; it has seven Par 3s, four Par 4s and a Par 5. There are at least half a dozen blind shots and some ingenious signalling devices to let players know when it is safe to play. In truth it is fun golf rather than serious golf but there is nothing wrong with that. It has also benefited in recent years from a new clubhouse which serves good homemade food (though doesn't have a licence). The distillery on Arran (called Arran

Distillery) is also quite distinctive being one of only two new distilleries opened in Scotland in the twenty year period from 1980-2000. It is privately owned and occupies new buildings at Lochranza in the north of the island. It is a smart looking distillery opened in 1995 by the Duke of Rothesay (otherwise known as The Prince of Wales) and boasts a very impressive visitor centre with a café (there is not much else in Lochranza!).

The geography of Campbeltown is perhaps surprising. The nearest Open course to Machrihanish is not Troon, Prestwick or Turnberry on the Ayrshire coast but Royal Portrush in Ulster on the Antrim coast. It is nearer Belfast than Glasgow. Campbeltown is south of Berwick-upon-Tweed so parts of England lie to the north of it. Now we can appreciate why it takes three hours to drive here!

There are just three remaining distilleries in Campbeltown but once there were as many as thirty before most closed down in the 1930s. My choice is the most famous, Springbank. The choice of golf course is not difficult; Machrihanish is widely accepted to be one of Scotland's classic links courses. That apart, the region is beautiful with much to recommend it for walking, sailing, fishing and wildlife.

To me the name 'Machrihanish' has a romance about it, suggesting a degree of proud history and remote splendour. It delivers on both counts. The course is the creation again of Old Tom Morris and apart from having what is widely accepted as one of the, if not the, world's greatest opening hole, (more on this later) it typifies everything about a 'classic Scottish links'; dramatic seaside location, 'out and back' layout with a few cross holes, dunes on the seaside nine and flatter ground on the 'inland' nine and wind always a factor.

A Barrel from Springbank Distillery

The Springbank distillery is the oldest distillery still to be privately owned by the original family. They have also recently re-opened a second distillery in the town – the Glengyle distillery. There is an interesting story about this; as Campbeltown used to have so many distilleries it justifiably had its own official 'whisky region' designation. However, after most had closed and only two remained, the Scotch Whisky Association some years back planned to remove the 'region' status from Campbeltown as it felt that just two distilleries did not merit it. This dispute encouraged the owners of Springbank to buy some old distillery buildings and build a new third distillery in the town so that Campbeltown could maintain its region status. The other distiller is also a small privately owned one, called Glen Scotia. Perhaps only Dufftown and Aberlour on Speyside have three great distilleries so close to each other.

Campbeltown is an ancient royal burgh and has connections to many famous figures from Scottish history from St Columba, who landed at Southend near the tip of the Mull and travelled through Campbeltown on his way to Iona, to Flora Macdonald, who allegedly set sail for America from the harbour, and Mary Campbell, one of Robert Burns' famous muses, known as 'Highland Mary' who lived there as a child. Today it is a pleasant small town which is beginning to re-invent itself. Its remoteness is a problem – there are only two daily flights to Glasgow from the small airport. However, as well as the whisky distilling, golf and tourism there remains a creamery producing excellent cheddar and while the famous herring fishing fleet is much reduced, shellfish have become the new focus. A few years ago there were only a couple of very average hotels but today the choice is much improved and there are also a number of smart Bed and Breakfast options.

Distant as it is, Campbeltown on the east side, or Machrihanish on the west, are still some 10 – 15 miles from the southern tip of the Mull. Campbeltown airport (maybe 'airport' is slightly overstating its status today) is in fact located on the west next to the Machrihanish golf courses. Today it has only two daily flights to Glasgow but as RAF Machrihanish it had a proud history. During the Second World War it boasted the largest runway in Europe, subsequently became an important NATO base for various Cold War activities and was the home to a US Navy Seal Commando Unit for a number of years. The airport was handed back to the MoD from NATO in 1995 and the MoD sold it in 2012.

There are now three courses at Machrihanish; the Old, the 9-hole Pans course and the new Machrihanish Dunes. The new course has been built to the north of the old course in a beautiful area of natural duneland. As the area is a Site of Special Scientific Interest (Machrihanish Bay has many rare species of shellfish) there were severe restrictions put upon the planning consent for a new course, so no earth was moved except for the greens. Most modern links, though they use the natural forms of the dunes, will move earth to help the design of the course. The new course is a delightful place but in terms of golfing experience, not in the same league as the Old – worth a visit but only as a supplement. To me, the main benefit of the new course is that its building has been accompanied by a renovation of the old Ugadale Hotel which had been derelict for many years. Its large, imposing Victorian structure had been a rather threatening and ghostly presence in the small hamlet. Today it has been made into accommodation along with neighbouring cottages; the format is rather 'American' and slightly contrived. The hotel is called 'The Kintyre Club' and the pub is called 'The Pub'. It is not my cup of tea but it is well marketed with the new Machrihanish Dunes course and if it brings visitors to this lovely area then it is to be applauded.

Machrihanish Golf Club is a traditional Scottish club with an adequate, but far from plush, clubhouse. As with a number of old clubs, the Ladies section has its own dedicated clubhouse adjacent to the Pans course. But the main experience here is the course and we should start with the first tee. Standing by the small Professional's Shop and looking across the bay to the course is one of the finest views in golf. Not that you can see much of the course which stretches its way along the coastline to the north. Here golf and the environment are as one. It is an attractive, wide, sweeping bay with an impressive Atlantic surf. The club motif is an oystercatcher and there are plenty to be seen bobbing up and down on the waves. To the north east there are the hills of the Mull where Paul McCartney had his house and you can immediately tell where his inspiration came from. You can imagine the 'mists rolling in from the sea.'

The club was initially formed in 1876 and was first a 10 and then a 12 hole layout. In 1879, with some new land acquired, they asked Old Tom Morris to advise on the extending of the course to 18 holes. Today's layout, including the famous first hole, dates from then and is largely Old Tom's creation.

As you cross the road and approach the Professional's Shop, which sits next to the first tee, you confront a stone with a plaque which simply states 'The best opening hole in the world'. A bold statement but one with which many people, me included, will concur. From a golfing perspective, it is indeed all, initially, about this extraordinary first hole; the famous 'drive across the Atlantic'. The name is apt because that is what you do. The hole is not particularly long (some 430 yards) but how long it plays depends on your drive. It is the ultimate risk and reward shot; the more of the bay you cut off, the shorter and easier the second shot. If you play conservatively, just over the corner of the bay you could be left with nearly 300 yards still to go. Perhaps you compromise and make sure that you have plenty club to cross the bay. The problem then is you might hit it too well and go over the fairway and into the rough, and conceivably into bunkers on the neighbouring 18th fairway. Oh the dilemmas! And then of course it depends on the wind direction, so the shot you played yesterday may not be right for today. The beach is in play but how much beach there is will depend on whether the tide is in or out. It is a wonderful hole, aesthetically and intellectually.

I have played the hole some six times. I have been once on the beach, from where I hit an impressive 7 iron back onto the fairway. I have been on the 18th fairway. I have several times been very conservative ending safely but still a good two shots away. But the last time I played, on a bright June evening, I hit my drive, which took off rather further left than I had intended. I had hit it well but the direction meant that I was trying to cut off more of the bay than I had planned. As the ball was in the air I was anxious. Would it make it? It landed about a foot over the beach just next to a marker post and hopped happily into the middle of the fairway leaving me just an 8 iron to the green. Only a golfer will understand the pleasure that shot gave me.

But Machrihanish is about more than its famous first hole. The second hole is unusual and difficult, with a blind uphill second shot over a stream to a severely undulating green. On that same June evening I hit my second shot up the hill and just made the summit, from where I hoped it might run down onto the green. But you only find the result when you walk up and I was delighted to see my ball nestling some 18 inches from the hole. Some days the golfing gods really are in your favour. No wonder I like Machrihanish! The third tee is one of the highest points on the course and gives a magnificent view across the course and back to the village. The hole itself is the first on a delightful stretch through the dunes and along the shore which makes up the front nine. As the second hole heads slightly inland, the third heads straight out to sea (it is fittingly called 'Islay', our next destination, which can be seen in the distance), downhill over a wonderfully natural bumpy fairway to a long narrow green. The fourth is a short hole with the green perched on top of a dune; it's easy if you hit the green but miss it at your peril. The next five Par 4s complete the front nine and are all memorable; dog-legs, uphill shots, downhill shots, greens placed perilously on top of dunes, others nestling in small dells. The direction of the holes shifts subtly so no two shots are the same; you will need every type of shot here.

The 9th green adjoins the airfield and then the course turns back. Holes 10 and 12 are two interesting Par 5s, the second with a hidden green amidst the dunes. Both 13 and 14 are tough Par 4s with tricky greens and these are followed by consecutive Par 3s, though the second one (rather scarily called 'Rorke's Drift') will require a driver for most of us. If the course has a weakness it is, as so often when a course is looking to find its way inland back to the clubhouse, 17 and 18, which have less character, though I am sure plenty of good rounds have come to grief on 17 where an enticing drive from an elevated tee is made all the harder by 'Out of Bounds' down the left-hand side.

A round at Machrihanish is a great experience. It is worth saying that of the nine courses featured in this book, Machrihanish would by most experts be rated the 'best' golf course. As I have said this is a very individual judgement but it will, almost without exception, appear in any list of the UK's Top 100 courses; in Scotland it would be in the Top 20, maybe the Top 10. As I have said, the criteria for appearing in this book are broader than just the quality of the golf course, but here it also delivers because of its wonderful location and because it is such an integral part of its location.

Before returning to Campbeltown to visit the distilleries it is worth taking the short trip down to the very end of the Mull of Kintyre to the appropriately named Southend village which itself has a very attractive golf course, Dunaverty. It is a combination of links and clifftop and, while not a top level course, the beauty is arresting looking out to the small isle of Sanda. When I visited, the course looked in good condition with the fairways firm, the semi- rough tidily cut and the main rough on some holes simply acres of bluebells. I'm not sure whether there is a local rule to prevent damage to such precious flora. There are delightful deserted beaches (the only life I saw on a bright June morning was an otter calmly strolling along the sea shore) and you can take a small road and climb within a few miles to over 1,000 feet, which gives you a view of the whole end of the peninsular.

Springbank is the oldest independent family-owned distillery in Scotland. Founded in 1828 by Archibald Mitchell it is now owned by his great, great, great, great grandson. J&G Mitchell & Co Ltd unusually produces three brands at the Springbank distillery (Springbank, Longrow and Hazelburn – all named after original Campbeltown distilleries) and also owns a second distillery in the town, Glengyle which was the first new distillery to be opened in Scotland after the millennium. It produces Kilkerran, a much peatier, 'Islay styled', single malt.

To visit Springbank you need to go the family-owned whisky shop called Cadenheads in Union Street and buy a ticket for one of the two daily tours. The shop is worth a nose around with each of the brands well displayed along with ranges of special bottlings. The distillery is a few hundred yards away up the street amongst an array of old Victorian buildings. Here you will not find a state-of-the art visitor centre. Springbank prides itself on its lack of sophistication. Indeed it relishes both its tradition and its old fashioned methods. Very little concession is given to modern ways; they joke about the 'computer over there' which proves to be a chalkboard. It is not a low cost operation as the distillery occupies a number of quite cramped buildings. But the whole process from floor maltings to bottling is done on site and there is considerable pride in this. It is probably the best place to see the traditional method of floor maltings in Scotland. The mill is an old Porteous mill; the kiln and use of peat is very manual; the mash tun is cast iron and solid; the washbacks are Swedish larch; the stills and spirit safes fairly old. The bottling plant is very manual; I think I counted about a dozen people on the bottling line. I suspect the high speed lines used by the multinationals in the central belt in Scotland might have two. But low cost is not what Springbank is about; the employment of local people in an industry which is so important to the town is a huge positive. The manual nature of the bottling also enables them to be flexible with small bottling runs. Cadenheads, like Gordon and McPhail in Elgin, produce special edition malts from various distilleries. They also bottle specialist gin and rum.

The Springbank distillery is unique in Scotland as it produces three single malt brands – normally a 'single malt' will have its own distillery. As well as Springbank, there is Hazelburn and Longrow. The process for each is distinct; as well as different times in the mash tun and levels of peat, Longrow is double distilled, Springbank has two and a half distillations, while Hazelburn is triple distilled.

The tour is very relaxed. Unlike at the big distilleries you can take as many photos as you like. The process is also conveniently spelled out on big boards. The tour can include a visit to the new Glengyle distillery which neighbours the Springbank site. This distillery could not be more different. It is housed in old distillery buildings but just one section has been devoted to the new distillery, in which brand new equipment has been installed. It is all very spick and span; a complete contrast from Springbank, but extraordinarily the distillery is only run for one month every year, during November, when the staff from Springbank move across and produce the Kilkerran brand in the new distillery. The rest of the year it is idle. This makes Kilkerran very rare and it therefore it commands a premium price.

Campbeltown's remoteness is challenging and the success of its golfing and whisky industries are crucial to the community's sustainability and prosperity. Fortunately both are magnificent examples and should have 'must visit' status on any tour of Scotland's golf and whisky destinations.

The Machrie Golf Club; 9th hole

The Par 3 9th is the best of the newly designed holes on the
Machrie. Not unlike the 8th at Kilspindie, it plays downhill
and looks straight out to sea with the wide sweep of Laggan Bay
and the south western tip of Islay visible in the distance.

The Mash Tun at Bunnahabhain Distillery
This is the second largest mash tun in Scotland, the largest
being at Glenfarclas on Speyside. It has a stainless steel sides
and a magnificent copper top and holds 12.5 tonnes.

CHAPTER NINE

Islay

'Don't play too much golf; two rounds a day is plenty'

Harry Vardon (1870-1937)
Six times winner of The Open. US Open Champion in 1900.

I MADE THE case for our first destination, Brora, to be the most beautiful (and there are many other candidates in between) but many will argue our final one, Islay, (pronounced '*isla*') should take that particular prize. It is a very special place with a wealth of wildlife and delightful scenery. Part of its charm is that it remains relatively undeveloped and unspoilt. This is because it is still not easy to travel there. Again, as with Machrihanish, there are just two flights a day from Glasgow to the small airport, while travelling by car involves at least one ferry trip. I definitely recommend this latter option, as arriving in Islay by ferry is part of the experience. There are two main options; Port Ellen in the south east and Port Askaig in the north, which takes you through the notorious Straights of Jura. On my most recent trip, I arrived at Port Askaig and left from Port Ellen and I recommend this as the best option. Both are served from Kennacraig, a small ferry terminal on the Mull about forty five minutes north of Campbeltown, just south of the small town of Tarbet. On the opposite side of the Mull, just a short drive away, there is also a ferry terminal at Claonaig which will take you over to Lochranza on the north coast of Arran, so there are different options as to how to get there. Close study of the Caledonian McBrayne timetable is strongly recommended.

Here the choice of golf course is not difficult as there is only one contender (the Machrie is the only course on the island) but by contrast the choice of distillery is very difficult as there are, despite the relatively small size of the island, no fewer than eight, plus two new ones planned. Islay is home to a number of famous malts, all with wonderfully romantic names which I enjoy reciting almost as much as I enjoy drinking their output; Ardbeg, Bowmore, Lagavulin, Laphroaig, Caol Ila, Bruichladdich, Bunnahabhain, Kilchoman… Which to choose? What a dilemma!

My last trip to Islay was on a calm June morning with not a cloud in the sky. The ferry trip from Kennacraig up the Sound of Jura, with Islay to the south and the much more mountainous Jura to the north, was magical; the scenery, the colours, the peace. I have been on ferry trips in the Mediterranean, the Aegean, in Sydney Harbour, San Francisco; give me Kennacraig to Port Askaig on a clear summer's day anytime. There is actually a golf course being built on Jura by an Australian entrepreneur who has bought the Ardfin Estate on the south end of the island overlooking the straights. I am not sure whether it is intended to be open to the public because there is very little public on Jura. It is much more sparsely populated than Islay which, at under 3,500, is itself not exactly overcrowded. Jura, however, has no towns and effectively just one road up the east coast. It is mainly known for its stag hunting and as the location where George Orwell wrote *1984*.

I will start with the golf. I first visited The Machrie in 2005 and have wonderful memories of it. The course was designed in 1890 by Willie Campbell, the golf professional at the Bridge of Weir club near Glasgow, who had grown up in Musselburgh as a contemporary of Willie Park Junior. He had regularly competed strongly in The Open but had never won it, losing by one stroke to Willie Park in 1897 and, like Park, was destined to emigrate to America where he became professional at the famous Country Club at Brookline and was responsible for upgrading the design of the course to a full 18 holes. He competed in the US Open in 1895, coming sixth, and the following year moved to another course, Myopia Hunt Club, which was to become a regular venue for the US Open in the early part of the 20th century. Sadly, he died prematurely in 1900 at the age of only 38.

The Machrie was a very unique layout. Willie Campbell had very much followed Donald Ross's dictum of following what God had laid out in the land and designed the holes amidst the natural hazards. In 2005 I counted 13 blind shots, so it was not a course for the purist. It lies in a vast area of duneland overlooking Laggan Bay in the south of the island just along from the airport. It is a delightfully beautiful spot with the wide bay and views to the famous Mull of Oa. After a fairly sedate start with a short Par 4 followed by a sweeping Par 5, where you drive across a burn, there then follows hole after hole which take the breath away. Each is memorable though a string of Par 4s from 6 to 9 probably stand out. The sixth is a marvellous hole where you drive blind down a hill to a narrow fairway from where you have a short but tricky pitch to the green. On the 7th tee there is no sight of any fairway, just a 50 ft high dune with a small post on top of it. You drive over it and hope for the best. If you are straight you will find your ball over the other side, from where you have another blind shot to a hidden green. The eighth is not a lot easier while 9 gives you two fairways to choose from, but both are very narrow.

The short 10th was probably the weakest hole on the course as it played out onto a wetland area by a burn and did not have a links feel. The 11th, however, immediately restored the quality of experience with a long par 4 to a narrow hidden green. The 12th was a tough Par 3 to a narrow green and 13 a delightful sweeping dog-leg Par 5 to a green set amidst the dunes. The last five holes were again all Par 4s but they all varied and all had tremendous character. All three of 14, 15 and 16 were perhaps relatively 'normal' but that can't be said of 17 where the green was completely hidden just over a high dune. The same was true on 18 which was in some ways reminiscent of the famous 17th at Prestwick with your second shot hit optimistically over another dune. It was in some way 'extreme' links golf where the elements play such a huge part in the outcome and in truth the element of fortune (good or bad) was perhaps too prevalent. But it was simply impossible not to be thrilled by the excitement of it all.

You will notice that the above description of the course is all in the past tense. It refers to the course in 2005. That is because the Machrie today is much changed. The club had had a difficult financial history. On my 2005 visit the hotel and self-catering cottages which overlooked the course were in a state of some disrepair. There was no proper clubhouse. The course was well looked after and in good condition (natural links courses do not require an enormous amount of maintenance) but everything else required investment.

The course and hotel were put up for sale a few years later. The problem was that nobody could come up with a business plan that would make it work. With a population of just 3,500 it could not rely on the local market but with only two flights a day by small planes, the potential for visiting golfers is also modest. Eventually it was sold and the new owner has undertaken to invest in it while maintaining the local club.

My surprise, visiting in the summer of 2016, was not to find that the investment was underway but that the immediate work had been undertaken on the course as opposed to the hotel, accommodation and clubhouse. In my view the course needed the least work while the hotel, when I visited, had become a pile of rubble and the club was being run from one of the old, rather unseemly, cottages. Meanwhile out on the course it was all change.

There was a case for some upgrading. I am not against courses moving with the times and some of the Machrie shots were a little too close to crazy golf. But any architect upgrading a course should respect its history and base the changes on the strengths of the old. The new Machrie, however, is simply a new course on the same land. While the new course follows broadly the same routing, there are very few holes that have not been radically altered in some respect; the 2nd and 4th are similar; the new 12th is essentially the same as the old 13th. But these exceptions apart, the new course is virtually unrecognisable from the old Machrie.

I believe that the new course, when it is completed (it was not fully so on my visit), will be a '*better*' course. It will be technically a very good course. But my question is simply this; 'Why?' Why destroy a marvellously distinctive old master and replace it with a superior new product? If the business plan is to compete with other big championship courses and become an important serious golfing venue then perhaps I could understand it. But this will never be the case. The danger is that the new Machrie will be just another good golf course in a very beautiful but quite inaccessible location. The old course was unique, not like any other course, and in this respect was as likely, or in my view *more* likely, to attract visitors as a result. I, and many others, would be more likely to make the trip to Islay to play the old distinctive Machrie than a new Machrie. Where the investment was needed was in the facilities; the hotel, the accommodation, the clubhouse.

The debate about changes to golf courses is one that will go on. I am not against it as technology has changed the game; even mid and high handicappers can hit the ball further than before and courses should adapt to the times. But there remain too many examples of change for change's sake. A number of other examples come to mind. The changes to the West Course at Wentworth are in my view a great shame. The 8th, 17th and 18th holes are no longer in character with the course that Harry Colt designed. There was a case for making amendments to all three holes. In each case the greens lacked a bit of 'presence' and definition. But they are now rather too contrived, with the stream in front of the 18th probably the best (or worst) example of this. Recently the Scottish Open was held at a famous old course; Royal Aberdeen. Some of the Professionals made comments and as a result a number of the greens have been upgraded. The 2nd and 3rd greens were both quite distinctive and eccentric. Now they are less so. Maybe they are 'better' but they are less memorable. Another example is in the United States at Scioto Country Club where Jack Nicklaus learnt to play. It was put through a modernisation programme in the 1970s. It ended up having two different designers for the front and back nine. I think the words of Jack Nicklaus himself describe my feelings: 'He did not restore the course, he redesigned it. It was still a nice course but not the course I had grown up with'.

I don't wish to be too critical. I think a visit to the new Machrie will be memorable and I would still urge anyone to go. The magnificent location will be the same; the quality of the turf will be the same (though actually with some of the earth-moving I saw, it won't be quite the same across the whole course.) The course will, I am sure, be a fantastic test of golf. Some of the new holes are indeed excellent; the replacement of the old Par 3 10th with a new Par 3 9th, which plays downhill to a green amidst the dunes just above the shoreline, is undoubtedly a huge improvement. The new 17th, which replaces the old 'hit and hope' over the dune with a sharp dog-leg, is also a good idea. But these changes could have been made without so much radical altering of the rest and keeping much of the distinctive quirkiness of the old.

It is much the same with brands of whisky. There is often a case for a change in the nature of the product, or the pack design. But beware the new Brand Managers who are out to make a name for themselves and see radical change as something which will get noticed. Generally malt whisky brands understand the importance of distinctiveness and are very protective of their history. The distinctive 'triangular' Glenfiddich bottle, or the dumpy Dalwhinnie bottle, are good examples of distinctive assets which these brands have maintained. Many of the designs are very classic and constrained, but it is possible with good design to modernise yet keep that look. The Glenlivet label, which has evolved subtly over the past few decades, is a good case history.

Apart from playing the Machrie and visiting the distilleries there is plenty to do on Islay. There are two RSPB Nature Reserves, both worth a visit. On the Oa peninsula in the south it is worth driving up from Port Ellen to a car park on the peninsula from where there is a magnificent cliff walk up to a monument commemorating two tragic events during the Great War when two American transport ships, the Tuscania and the Otranto, sank on the rocks off the coast of the island. Over 200 hundred lives were lost in the two disasters, the latter happening just a month before the Armistice. It is an impressive monument in a wonderful location. From the walk along the cliffs you can see golden eagles and a range of other bird-life. I also saw wild, white goats on the cliffs when I visited.

Then on the east side of the island is Loch Guinart which is very different in style. The walk up onto the moors delivers much gentler scenery, but again the birdlife is impressive and the setting marvellously peaceful. Elsewhere there are many other walks, and nowadays there is a much greater choice of quality accommodation and food.

So how do I choose one distillery on Islay? I've decided it is not possible. On this occasion I am not going to suggest just one because if you have an interest in whisky and have made the effort to travel to Islay it would be a shame to visit just one distillery. The eight existing distilleries are effectively in three areas; Ardbeg, Lagavulin and Laphroaig on the east coast, Bowmore, Bruichladdich and Kilchoman in the centre and south, and Caol Isla and Bunnahabhain in the north.

The three east coast distilleries are situated just north of Port Ellen and lie next door to each other occupying beautiful positions overlooking the coast. All three of these distilleries produce strongly peated malts, which generally Islay is famous for. Laphroaig is usually considered the most peaty – I find it much too strong tasting for my liking but it is probably the one malt whisky I could definitely name in a blind tasting. Lagavulin is also strongly peaty but in my view rather richer and sweeter as well. Of the three, Ardbeg has the smartest visitor centre and is the most geared up for visits. The buildings have been beautifully restored and, as well as an extensive shop, there is an excellent restaurant. It is very professionally done and it is therefore not a surprise that it is owned, like Glenmorangie, by LMVH. This is an international luxury brands business which has given Ardbeg the full treatment. Lagavulin (Diageo) and Laphroaig (Suntory) are also multi-nationally owned as are Bowmore and now Bruichladdich which, having been closed down in 1993 by White and Mackay (at that time owned by Jim Beam Brands), was bought by an English entrepreneur in 1990, who brought it back to life and sold it on for a handsome return to Remy Cointreau (yes, more French interest) in 2012.

While I would recommend visiting at least one in each area the two I am going to feature are Kilchoman and Bunnahabhain; the former representing the renewed interest in Islay malts and the latter one of the old established businesses which gave Islay its unique reputation.

Kilchoman is a new distillery situated in the south west of the island on a farm. It is very much a small scale, family-owned, farm distillery and is marketed as such. Indeed the family have recently purchased the farm as well (they were previously just renting some of the buildings). It is worth a visit for many reasons; the tour is very good and the small scale enables them to demonstrate the whole process, from floor malting to bottling, very clearly. The floor maltings are very small as only about 20 per cent of their limited output uses barley from Islay which goes into their *100% Islay* brand. For the majority of their production they bring in the malted barley in the same way as the other Islay distilleries.

Bunnahabhain Distillery

They have also taken a decision not to wait ten years to make their single malts. Clearly this presents an enormous cash flow challenge so they decided to market a range of non-age denominated brands most of which will be relatively 'young'. Their core line is Machir Bay and has a distinct 'Islay style' with a hint of 'peatiness'. The business has limited capacity and will have difficult decisions to make in managing their stocks as their sales have clearly exceeded expectations. Perhaps this explains why there are plans for another two new distilleries to be built on Islay, one at Gartbreck, south of Bowmore, and one at Loch Ardnahoe, a beautiful location in the north near Port Askaig. The former, which planned to use 'live flame' heating of the stills, Oregon pine washbacks, traditional worm tub condensers and slow distillation, is now under threat as a result of a land dispute, while the latter is being built by the independent bottlers Hunter Laing (who incidentally own the strip of land which has caused the Gartbreck plan to stall).

The visitor centre at Kilchoman includes a pleasant café and is clearly an important part of the business. It is impressively laid out with the accompanying gift shop selling an extensive range of goods from branded clothing to the usual glasses and memorabilia. In fact the one thing that jarred for me was the extent of 'stuff' being sold in the shop, from Danish pottery (why?) to plastic children's toys imported from China. To me this rather spoilt what was otherwise an impressively marketed brand.

Kilchoman is an enjoyable and worthwhile visit but I feel that given the history and reputation of Islay as a whisky destination, it should not itself represent the island and a visit here should be supplemented by a visit to an old established distillery as well. For this I have chosen Bunnahabhain which lies on the north coast, just west of Port Askaig. I have a number of reasons for choosing Bunnahabhain, which is pronounced *Boo-na-ha-vin* (it takes a while to learn this, never mind spell it).The business is owned by Distell Group, a South African drinks business which also owns the Tobermory and Deanston distilleries. There are many arguments for not choosing it: the product is probably not a typical Islay malt, being probably the 'least peaty' on the island. The distillery buildings are not beautiful and are indeed in need of some renovation. And the 'visitor centre' is a rather scruffy, 15 ft square room up a narrow outdoor staircase. However, its location is second to none, overlooking a pretty bay with magnificent views of Jura. It is an extraordinarily peaceful spot; I sat on a wall above the stony beach looking out across the bay towards Jura and all I could hear was a very gentle lapping of the water onto the shore and the faint chugging of the Colonsay ferry passing in the distance. And while the buildings are not elegant they have a certain Victorian grandeur about them. Here I can truly understand why Barnard made a case for a distillery's location being part of its brand. Previously, when trying a Bunnahabhain, I had always simply envisaged a point on the map in the north of Islay. In future every sip will be accompanied by the memory of this extraordinarily pretty setting. The atmosphere is also very relaxed and friendly. For my June visit I was given an exclusive tour by a very knowledgeable and enthusiastic young lady guide. She was very passionate about the brand and her job – she was not just going through the motions which can be the impression with some of the tours at the larger distilleries. The highlight of the tour here is probably 'the second biggest mash tun in Scotland' which is indeed an impressive sight. (For the record, the largest is at Glenfarclas on Speyside).They also boast the tallest stills on Islay, giving them more copper contact and therefore, in their view, a distinctive product.

Their main products are 12-, 18-, and 25-year-old malts, while they also produce some special edition, more peaty lines. Their other claim to distinctiveness is that they mature all their product on site, mainly in dunnage warehouses, which they claim gives their product its distinctive flavour from the sea air. I questioned this, but my delightful guide was insistent it was true. Well, obviously the barrels breathe and so the local air combines with the product but does it really have an impact on the taste of the end product? Does it actually matter whether or not it does? The thought that it might is enough. Maybe the fact that the barrels are matured in such a delightful and peaceful location imbues the spirit with additional mellowness.

While the Machrie is perhaps not the ideal golf course to finish the book on, I think Bunnhabhain is a good place to end the whisky tour. It is an old established brand; the distillery is in a delightful location; the business, being internationally owned, is an example of the global appeal of the product, while the whisky itself promotes its own distinctive characteristics.

The Bunnahabhain claim that the sea air during its maturation is an important feature of their product is yet another example of the mysteries of malt whisky. Clearly every brand in such a crowded market is looking for distinctive characteristics and the product itself, being, on the one hand so simple (just three permitted ingredients), but on the other so complex, lends itself to this. All malt whisky is made from the same 'recipe of ingredients' but sample a Laphroaig or a Lagavulin and then a Glenkinchie or a Bunnahabhain, and even a newcomer to whisky will recognise that they taste a world apart. Explaining why gives every brand its own story and its own unique position in the market. The mystique is more important than the truth and that is a very good summary of what I have learnt about malt whisky.

Afterword

THIS IS NOT a book for wide-ranging conclusions but I think some reflection is in order. The question I am most asked about both whisky and golf is 'What is your favourite whisky/golf course?' I never give an answer and I won't pronounce on my favourites within this book because the question misunderstands my relationship with both. To me it is an impossible question to answer and I would give different responses at different times; the beauty of both lies in their variety. I wouldn't want a favourite of either; just as I would never want only to play just one golf course for the rest of my life, equally I would never just drink one brand of whisky. I have courses and brands I like a lot, others I like a bit less and others I tend to avoid, but I have a long list of favourites of each. It's the Desert Island Discs problem; having to choose just eight pieces of music is difficult enough, but choosing just one to save feels impossible.

Whisky and golf have so many other similarities; the centrality of the local landscape in dictating a particular whisky or golf course's character; the parallel histories of the two over the past two centuries and their global popularity today; the delicate balance of needing to adapt to the modern world while holding onto some traditions; the importance of context in the enjoyment of both.

I have been struck by how both whisky and golf are products of both nature and man. Two of the famous figures in the development of both make this point. Masataka Taketsuru, the founder of the Japanese whisky industry who served his apprenticeship at Hazelburn distillery in Campbeltown saw whisky making as 'an act of cooperation between the blessings of nature and the wisdom of man', while Donald Ross, the Dornoch born architect of so many of America's great early courses, famously said the 'God made golf holes; it is the duty of the architect to find them.' Great whiskies and great golf courses are both products of Scottish human ingenuity in exploiting Scottish natural assets. And while a great distillery or a great golf course does not actually need to be located in spectacularly beautiful surroundings, somehow it adds to the positive experience of both.

My reflections on whisky are many. The industry seems in good health with a surge of investment from both home and abroad going into new distilleries. World demographics (a growing middle class in developing economies) support the business cases for these investments. Yet, in Scotland the future lies in the premium product, malt whisky, and the distinctiveness of its products and brands.

Golf is perhaps in less good health. The number of regular players is falling both in the UK and particularly in the United States. It still has an image of being rather elitist and 'stuffy' while it also suffers from the essential paradox of modern life; the more we invent things which allow us to do everything more quickly and conveniently, the less time we seem to have to enjoy life. A sport that can take over half a day (including travel to a course) is not tailored to the demands of today's restless consumer. Yet at the top of the game the rewards are greater than ever and, despite the declining number of players in some established countries, the game is growing in Asia and golf clubs in many towns, particularly in Scotland and Ireland, still act as important centres of the local community.

What I have learned most about malt whisky is how important distinctiveness is and how each brand recognises the need to market what differentiates it from others. I had always known that there were differences from the smoky Islay malts to the milder Lowland ones but I had not fully understood what caused these differences. It is remarkable that such a heavily regulated product, with only three permitted ingredients, can produce such radically different end results. I have been told of so many factors that cause this and I have concluded two things; first, that technically the most important factor, by a long way, is the maturation and, secondly, the marketing story which focuses on a particular trait of a particular brand can be just as important. A well marketed myth can be as powerful as a technically proven reality. That is the beauty of malt whisky; it can on the one hand be strictly defined through its legal definition but the end product can still be endlessly varied. And much of that variety can be in the taste buds and mind of the drinker.

Just as Scotland has a central role in the marketing of whisky, Scotland is world-renowned as the country that invented golf. St Andrews now markets itself as 'the Home of Golf' but in truth the whole of Scotland can do this. The major Open venues in Scotland from St Andrews to Carnoustie, Muirfield, Troon and Turnberry are world famous and attract visitors from all around the globe. Yet Scotland's fame can be used by the rest of the country. All the courses I have chosen have considerable history and can claim to be part of the development of a sport that has grown in popularity globally.

It started in America, which became the main driver of the game for over half a century, often with Scottish architects leading the way, but more recently it has grown in Europe and in particular in the Far East. I feel the smaller clubs need to do more to market their distinctiveness. The elite clubs, the Open venues, are perhaps the equivalent of the multinational whisky brands. Their reputations are established. Yet, just as the smaller whisky brands have become adept at finding their own distinctive story, there is an opportunity for the smaller, less famous golf clubs to create their own niche. Brora does this, being the home of the James Braid Golfing Society; Tain and Moray should perhaps make more of being Old Tom Morris designs; Rosemount has a number of angles it could promote, while Machrihanish can proudly claim to have the best opening hole in the world. Some are better than others at marketing their distinctiveness; everything from the clubhouse welcome to the design of the website and the scorecard. The health of the whisky market is that there is room for both elite multinational brands as well as the smaller players. In whisky many enthusiasts eschew the bigger, more famous distilleries in favour of the smaller, niche ones. Golf needs to be the same. Visitors will flock to the famous courses but many miss out on playing the less known ones which would often, particularly for mid and higher handicap players, be at least as good an experience for them.

Golf has suffered from an image of being elitist. Yet this is changing. In many communities the golf club is in fact very democratic where people from all walks of life share a passion. Golf as a game has also the advantage, as I stated in the preface, of enabling beginners to compete alongside elite players. Some golf clubs have a bad reputation of being not only elitist but also ageist and sexist, but in truth in the vast majority of clubs there are very active ladies' and men's sections, regular mixed competitions and strong support for juniors. Also, most of the more arcane 'dress code' rules have been relaxed, though some clubs rightly set their own standards. I think the game itself will also adapt; just as cricket has introduced shortened formats of the game, so too golf will have to evolve its formats. As I said, 9 hole competitions are now being encouraged while there is even a new 6 hole format which cannot take more than one hour, with players given only 30 seconds to complete each shot. This may also help speed up the pace of play generally.

Whisky has never had an elitist reputation though malt whisky being a premium priced product is certainly not mainstream. Many of the distilleries are also very much part of the local community and are seen as important both in creating employment and attracting visitors. The employees at the distilleries are almost universally local or at least Scottish. Those working in production, from those who run the process to the master blenders, are all highly skilled. Those who work in the visitor centres selling the brand and giving the tours are not generally slick marketing executives but proud and enthusiastic locals. I found, particularly in the smaller distilleries, there was always a real passion for the brand and the product with a strong team spirit evident.

But above all, I think what connects whisky and golf the most, and what most reflects their essential 'Scottishness', is best summed up in Arnold Palmer's description of golf; they are both 'deceptively simple and endlessly complicated'. I now realise that like famous wines of different vintages, no batch even of a leading brand (e.g. Glenmorangie 12 year old) will be exactly the same. It is like a pint of your favourite draft beer; it won't taste exactly the same each time. With beer we accept that each pint may differ slightly because of its age or how it has been kept and handled, but somehow when a dram of whisky comes out of a bottle we assume it will be exactly the same as the last dram you had out of a different bottle. Every Mars Bar or can of Coca Cola will be the same as it is made to a tight technical specification. The same cannot be true of a malt whisky. To me that is a positive; it is what makes whisky so interesting and is one of the attractions of drinking it. As Iain Banks concludes in his book exploring whisky; 'There is of course, no perfect dram. Or there are lots, depending on how you look at it. What apparently tastes like a perfect dram now might not taste so good later. What tastes like a brilliant dram to me might taste awful to you.' He is right; if you want absolute certainty, it is not the drink for you.

Golf is also not a game of absolute certainty. It was Bobby Jones, arguably the greatest ever golfer, who uniquely achieved the 'grand slam' winning both the Amateur Championships and the Opens in both the US and Great Britain in the same year, 1930, who said that 'golf is the closest game to the game we call life. You get bad breaks from good shots; you get good breaks from bad shots'. Any golfer knows that you have good rounds and bad rounds. You can enjoy the same course one day and not the next. The reason for this can be that the course conditions have changed (the weather perhaps or how short the green keeper has cut the greens) or, more likely, it could be that you have changed and you have played well one day and badly the next. I have frequently looked forward to a round on a course I like; I am feeling confident, the weather is perfect, the companionship good. But then I play badly and come off with a slight sense of disappointment. Or sometimes, having played poorly for a week or two, I set off low on confidence in less-than-perfect weather and find that everything clicks into place and I end the round elated. Indeed, your mood will also affect your enjoyment of a dram of malt whisky. Even a dram from the same bottle might taste particularly good one day and not so the next, depending on how you feel, what you have just eaten or your general emotional state. Sometimes you have a whisky and it is just a whisky. Other times it feels more than that. It is all about context.

But isn't this just life? Often what you look forward to most will disappoint, while real joy is so often unexpected. And here whisky and golf have yet another connection; they both represent life itself. They can be delightful, intriguing, ever-changing, sometimes disappointing, relaxing, perhaps surprising, often frustrating, frequently obsessing and always beguiling. Certainly, they are never uninteresting.

Andrew Brown
November 2017

remote locations, there are also city distilleries planned in both Glasgow and Edinburgh. So, as you can see, there is activity the length and breadth of the country. And this investment is not just in smaller micro-distilleries; there are new distilleries being created by the big players. Diageo's Roseisle distillery in Moray, opened in 2009 and has a capacity of 12.5 million litres, and Dalmunach, from Chivas Brothers, opened in 2015 and has a capacity of 10 million litres, while the Edrington Group is investing in an architecturally innovative new distillery at Macallan to meet its growth ambitions for this famous Speyside brand. For a version of the 'back nine' there would be plenty of potential in combining some of these sites with interesting golf courses - indeed the opening of a micro-distillery at the Castle Hotel in Dornoch is surely a perfect excuse to go back and play that wonderful course again.

But having learned what I did in Scotland, I think to explore both 'pastimes' more; I should move beyond Scotland and investigate how they are faring elsewhere. Golf soon spread from its beginnings in Scotland to the rest of the United Kingdom and Ireland and thence to America in the late 19th century. Whisky also spread across the world, to America and Japan in particular, but within the United Kingdom was initially only produced in Ireland. Indeed, in the late 19th century the industry was as famous in Ireland as it was in Scotland, but it went into severe decline during the first half of the 20th century and the early years of independence. I welcome the opportunity to understand why this happened. For a long time there were only three distilleries but fortunately, if gradually, the industry has re-established its reputation and, over the past ten years in particular, there have been many new developments. England

and Wales never had a whisky tradition but this is now also changing and we now see openings in a number of regions and I want to understand why this has taken so long. I am also keen to learn whether golf is regarded differently across the country. Admittedly, outside Scotland the link with whisky is tenuous so my locations will to an extent be driven by the location of the distilleries.

As I enjoyed so many beautiful locations on my Scottish tour, I have used location as one of the criteria for deciding where to visit. I have chosen four in England with quite a wide geographical spread between them, one in Wales, one in Northern Ireland and three in the Irish Republic. In England and Wales, I have deliberately chosen courses that have an association with Scotland – which is not difficult because so many of the great ones have this. In Ireland the courses have more of an Irish heritage, although this golfing heritage was also heavily influenced, like its whiskey industry, by Scotland.

So what is the point of whisky outside Scotland? Is it just a poor relation? Irish whiskey (yes, it has an 'e' in Ireland) has a justifiable reputation but will English or Welsh whisky ever match the reputation of the product produced by their famous neighbour? And is there the same passion for the product that you find north of the border?

It is worth remembering that Scotch is now a minnow in the world of whisky. The global market is dominated by Indian whisky though this is a very different product from either blended Scotch or Scotch malt whisky. Indeed the very definition of whisky is debateable since Scotch is governed by fairly tight regulations whereas elsewhere in the world regulations are either much looser or non-existent. I will ponder whether this is a strength or a weakness for traditional Scotch because, potentially, it will allow new players distilling outside of Scotland to offer more innovative products. And the world of whisky is a growing one, with both the market growing and new distilleries opening across the world and thus increasing the total number, and with many countries developing their own whisky industries. It is a bit like wine where the established producers (France, Italy and Spain) have, over the past thirty years, faced increasing competition from 'New World' wines; 'New World' whiskies (which will also come from some 'Old World' countries such as France, Germany, Sweden and Austria) will undoubtedly play an increasingly important part in the market over the next thirty years and the number of 'New World' producers will be much greater than for wine because the constraints of climate are not so significant. As countries develop their own whisky industries, it will be interesting to see which particular countries can create a reputation for a distinctive product. How will Scotch fare against such rapidly increasing competition? As I visit England, Wales and Ireland it will be interesting to see how the new ventures are positioning themselves. How will they distinguish themselves from Scotch whisky or do they see themselves as just part of a global trend and their geographical proximity to Scotland as merely coincidental?

In golf it is instructive to understand how the game changed when it moved south of the border, which it did very quickly from the 1890s. There are clearly more courses and golfers in England but golf does not have the same 'market share' of sport as it has in Scotland and the number of courses per head of population is much smaller. I mention in *Of Peat and Putts* that the Island of Arran with a population of about five thousand people has seven golf courses; three with eighteen holes, three with nine holes and the famous twelve-hole course at Shiskine. That is ninety-three golf holes on an island approximately twelve miles by five miles – it would be possible for thirty per cent of the entire population of Arran to play golf on the same day! In England there is much more competition from other sports and, as I mention, golf is facing some challenges in adapting to modern lifestyle trends – put simply, it takes too long to play. Whisky, on the other hand, is becoming increasingly popular hence the distillery openings in England and many other countries. Whisky has the benefit that it is part of an artisan food and drink trend that includes a wide range of food and drink categories from cheeses, to breads, to beer and, most recently, spirits. Among the spirits gin is leading the way because it can be brought more quickly to market and has, perhaps, a younger image. I will examine the influence of gin which is rapidly overtaking whisky in popularity and the increasing trend, also prevalent in Scotland, of producing whisky in a distillery alongside gin and vodka. The business advantages are clear but can this generalist approach ever produce the same passion for product quality of the focused whisky producer?

My tour will encompass first, England and Wales, and then will move to Ireland. We will start in The Lake District, move across to the east coast of Yorkshire down to Norfolk and Suffolk and then to Devon in the west country. Pendyrn, Wales's most famous distillery, is handily placed near the south Pembrokeshire coast where the choice of golf courses is rich and from there it is easy to take the ferry from Fishguard to

Ireland. The four distilleries that I have chosen in Ireland occupy almost the four corners of the island, starting with Dublin area, moving up to the Antrim coast in Northern Ireland, round to Donegal and then to the Kerry peninsular in the far south west. Arguably Ireland, unlike England and Wales, with its strong whisky heritage, deserves more scrutiny but the four distilleries I have chosen represent a good cross-section of the industry and will enable me to explore the traditions of Irish whiskey and how it differs from that of its Celtic neighbour.

I am continually astonished at the number of books on whisky from extremely knowledgeable people and I should remind the reader that the 'back nine' will be for amateur enthusiasts rather than experts. I am probably more discerning about my golf courses than my whiskies because I have been playing golf for over fifty years yet drinking whisky for only ten years, yet I am keen to learn more; my comments on the product should be seen in this context. Whatever, there is always more to learn and that is one of the product's beauties. Perhaps there is less innovation in golf, but it also has made some interesting developments in course design and course upkeep, generally improving the quality of players' experiences.

There is a universe in whisky and golf. As soon as I finished *Of Peats and Putts* and having seen vistas unroll before me, I had an uncontrollable thirst to discover and learn more. I hope that the same is true at the conclusion of this one and that I can infect you with some of my passion.